Managerial Problem Solving

Charles J. Margerison
Bradford University Management Centre

London · New York · St Louis · San Francisco · Düsseldorf ·
Johannesburg · Kuala Lumpur · Mexico · Montreal · New Delhi
Panama · Paris · São Paulo · Singapore · Sydney · Toronto

Published by

McGRAW-HILL Book Company (UK) Limited
MAIDENHEAD · BERKSHIRE · ENGLAND

Library of Congress Cataloging in Publication Data

Margerison, Charles.
    Managerial problem solving.

    (McGraw-Hill European series in management)
    1. Communication in management. 2. Meetings. 3. Problem solving.
I. Title.

HF5718.M37   658.4'51   74-10901
ISBN 0-07-084445-3

For my Mother, Violet Margerison –
a most creative manager and problem solver

CONTENTS

PREFACE

'The trouble with my subordinates is that they are not as skilled as they could be in managing other people. As technical specialists in their particular area, whether it be finance, marketing, production, or other areas, my managers are very sound. However, they do not seem able to communicate with fellow colleagues and subordinates.

'It's not that they are lost for words. Most of them are highly articulate. It's just that the words they use, and the way they use them, have the opposite effect of what they are trying to achieve. More often than not, people resist their attempts at influence. The result is that the job doesn't get done on time, poor-quality work is turned out, and absenteeism and labour turnover are too high.

'I can see the problem, but in many ways I am in the same boat. What should I and others do to get work done here by improving the way we manage people?'

This book concentrates on providing some ideas and approaches that managers and others might consider trying out to deal with a problem such as the one posed above.

My attention was drawn to this problem by many managers, and it was expressed in many different ways. Some put forward the problem as lack of motivation in their subordinates, others defined it as a lack of creativity, others referred to the need for leadership skills, while others mentioned communication problems. On discussing the matter, a common theme usually began to emerge, which centred on the importance of the manager's task as a group leader.

Managerial Coordination and Integration

In the role of group leader, a manager has to integrate the work of many people. His skill lies primarily in bringing together and coordinating the work of others. However, few people in their professional or on-the-job training are specifically taught such skills. They have to pick them up by trial and error. While trials are vital, it is important to reduce the amount of error.

Managerial Problem Solving

What, then, does managerial coordination and integration mean? In the terms set out in this book, we shall refer to it as the skills of *managerial problem solving*. This involves bringing subordinates and/or colleagues together in various groups of different size to solve joint problems related to work tasks.

Our focus is, therefore, on the talks and discussions managers have with other people. Talking with others is a basic, and often overlooked, skill of the manager. When you talk with others, do they listen or just switch off? How much influence do you have when putting forward your ideas? How effective are you at responding to what other people say and do?

The approach used is to present some ideas which can aid our understanding of managerial problem solving, and then test them in the context of case examples. An attempt is made throughout to apply the concepts and ideas to practical day to day managerial problems.

The book, therefore, is about managers resolving problems (and that explicitly includes identifying and exploiting opportunities) in discussion with others. This involves technical and behavioural considerations. The emphasis here will be mainly on the behavioural factors.

Throughout the book, two important phrases will recur which are an integral part of managerial problem solving. The first is *group problem solving*. This is the part of managerial problem solving which puts the emphasis on the nature and type of group used in the problem solving process. How many people will be involved, and what sort of meeting will be held? This issue is taken up in chapter 1. The second is *interpersonal problem solving*. This also refers to managerial problem solving but it explicitly refers to the interaction between people.

What is Inside?

The structure of the book is as follows:

Chapters 1 to 6 identify the relationship between problems, solutions, and managerial action. In these chapters, the basic ideas of the book are set out and related to case examples. The names used in the case incidents are all fictitious, although the incidents themselves have foundations in organizational life.

Chapters 7 to 11 extend these ideas and try to show what sort of responses and behaviour emerge in various managerial problem-solving situations.

Chapters 12 to 15 take up specific themes in the management of people and treat each in some depth. Chapter 12 examines the possible consequences when managers use punishment as a strategy to deal with people and problems. In contrast, chapter 13 goes to the opposite end of the scale and looks at some possible outcomes when managers seek to use help as a strategy for dealing with people and problems. Chapters 14 and 15 again deal with both sides of a similar coin. The chapter entitled 'Getting Cornered' illustrates the pitfalls of the manager who is pinned down by his colleagues and subordinates on a particular issue, to which they object. The subsequent chapter 'Conversational Seduction' examines the problem in a meeting where the discussion is taken from one point to another without anything being achieved or decided.

Finally, chapter 16 seeks to draw together some threads and provide some broad guideline for managers who are specifically concerned to improve their business meetings and managerial problem-solving skills.

It has not been the aim to provide a literature review, with pages of references, but rather an easy-to-read book of ideas for the person who is primarily interested in trying them out in practice.

All books are an amalgam of personal experience, and the work of others. In this last particular, I have gained considerably from the written work of Lord Wilfred Brown who structured my thinking about managerial meetings. I have also learnt a lot from the work of Professor Norman F. Maier whose example as a management educator was of considerable importance in stimulating this book. Beyond that, I have learnt from managers of their world, their problems, and the need for solutions and effective action. This is a difficult world, for there are many variables to be juggled with simultaneously. Managers are often criticized, which, given their complex task, is easy to do. It is difficult to manage effectively, and it is hoped this book will help managers to do so.

The book was written off and on over a two-year period, during which time I was sustained and encouraged by my wife Colinette, who provided the home conditions both in Brussels and Baildon necessary for thought. To my daughter Jill and son Alan, thanks for your smiling faces, and patient understanding on the occasions you came to see what I was doing.

Charles J. Margerison
Baildon
May 1974

INTRODUCTION

To whom did you last speak before you opened this book? What did you say? How did the other person respond? How far did the meeting achieve your objectives and those of the others present?

This book is about what you and everyone else does each day of their lives. It concentrates on what happens when we meet and talk. How successful are we in our interactions? In what way do we seek to improve our personal communication?

The focus is primarily on how people relate with and to each other when there is a problem at hand. The principles outlined have general application, but it is written primarily for managers, and the case incidents reflect the world of the production, marketing, financial, and other managerial functions.

While I recognize that structural factors such as roles and technology determine behaviour I have confined the present work to interpersonal and procedural issues in problem solving.

It is important that I state at the outset that I am here concerned with people getting together in duos, trios, quartets or any size of group to resolve problems through discussion. There are no golden formulae, but there are guidelines.

Managerial problem solving is about the interpersonal processes of the subject and the procedures. It is concerned above all to identify alternative lines of managerial action from which people can choose.

1

MANAGERIAL MEETINGS FOR PROBLEM SOLVING

MANAGERS AND MEETINGS

Imagine you are a manager confronted by the following problem. One of your subordinates, Jim Robinson, who has worked in the department for just over six months, has started coming to work late, taking off half-days, saying he is not feeling well, and generally not working hard. He has been late seven times during the last month, including three times this week.

You have considered the alternative ways of dealing with this problem. The following are the major approaches you feel you could use:

1. Call Robinson into your office and tell him you are concerned about his lateness, absenteeism, and standard of work and try to work out a mutually agreeable solution.

2. Talk with Robinson and suggest to him that if he improves his time-keeping, attendance record, and quality of work you will recommend him for a rise at the end of the year.

3. Invite Robinson to your office and ask him what the reasons are for his lateness, absenteeism, and poor-quality work, but suspend any decisions till a later date.

4. Take the issue to the next works council meeting. At the meeting, try to get a decision from the representatives of managers and operatives that if an employee is late at least six times in a month he should be liable for dismissal.

5. Tell Robinson that he has infringed the work rules regarding lateness and absenteeism and that you are deducting a half-day's pay in respect of these offences. Also tell him you are moving him to a less demanding job till the quality of his work improves.

Each of the five alternatives would involve a different kind of meeting. We shall examine, in this chapter, the various kinds of meetings managers can construct to deal with day to day interpersonal relations problems. In subsequent chapters, we shall explore the behaviour that managers, their colleagues, and their subordinates can and do develop in these meetings; what sort of meetings are appropriate and what sort of behaviour is likely to be most effective in resolving problems between people at work.

Before analysing the above problem, let us look at some other problems that can and do occur at work.

Imagine you are a works manager. You have twenty supervisors and nearly three hundred employees. One of the supervisors has just informed you that the shop stewards are planning to restrict output during the day in order to gain overtime.

Alternatively, consider that you are a sales manager. The sales during the last year have dropped by ten per cent. Of the twelve salesmen who report to you, only six have earned commission during the year. Your boss, the general manager, has just talked to you and stressed that the situation must improve quickly.

Finally, put yourself in the position of the research manager. You feel that there is insufficient emphasis on the practical application of research among your staff. Too many of them in your opinion enjoy doing pure research. The managing director has made it clear that the firm must have two new products within a year's time. You have thought up a couple of ideas that could be commercially worth while. But you are not sure they would be of interest to your staff as work problems.

Here are just four situations confronting different types of managers. Such problems occur in varying shades and emphasis in different organizations from time to time. The central problem on each occasion for the manager in question is 'What should I do?'

The manager would find it difficult, if not impossible, to resolve such problems by himself. Indeed, his task as a manager is to discuss the issues with others who are involved. Therefore, the manager in such situations as those described has to decide with whom he should talk to overcome the difficulty. Of equal importance, he must also consider *what kind of meeting* he should hold. We shall return to the above case problems as we proceed through the chapter.

MANAGERIAL TIME AND WORK

Managers spend most of their time at work in discussion with other people on how to resolve joint problems. Research clearly indicates that between

65 and 80 per cent of most managers' time is spent with one or more people in meetings.

The research only confirms what we know from our own experience. How many times have we rung up someone, only to have a secretary at the other end of the line say Mr X is unavailable at present because he is in a meeting? Our own work day is punctuated by meetings. They may be planned formal meetings, such as a committee, or a chance informal meeting with someone in the lift or corridor.

All the time, business is being transacted in these meetings; information is being exchanged, problems outlined, ideas shared, decisions made, advice offered, and instructions given. Some of these meetings are a waste of time, others are highly productive. A central issue is, therefore, how can a manager's time in meetings, which constitute on average two-thirds of his work, be made more effective? The ideas expressed here aim to provide guidance for managers on the behaviour they need to adopt if they are to achieve improved results from business meetings.

A Managerial Problem-Solving Focus

When people try to define managerial work, the phrase 'getting things done through working with other people' is often mentioned. While this is obviously too simple a definition, it does emphasize the importance of working with others. Occupying a managerial role implies that the manager leads or guides the work of others who have a relationship to him in the organization. It is the manager's task to coordinate and orientate their work towards particular objectives. In this job the manager, regardless of his particular function, will inevitably be involved with basic problems of how to influence the behaviour of others. The problems that a manager has to consider with others include:

• How can the approach of employees to their work and productivity be discussed?

• How can the discussion of introducing new work methods be tackled?

• How should a meeting with an employee who has broken company rules be conducted?

• How can mutually satisfactory objectives between the manager and the managed be attained?

• How should a manager discuss with his subordinates their work performance?

Most of these issues are of day to day concern to most managers; and the overall performance of a manager will depend on the way he manages the factors involved. These problems can be resolved through the process of what we shall here refer to as *managerial problem solving*—or MPS.

Managerial problem solving can be approached in a systematic manner which can improve a manager's effectiveness in meetings, and we intend to outline the principles and processes involved in doing this. The focus here, therefore, is to identify the factors associated with developing effective group problem-solving managerial behaviour and exploit opportunities. A part of this is discussion between people and we shall therefore examine interpersonal factors as well as procedures and organization structures. The prime emphasis will be on the face to face discussions between managers and others, which we shall sometimes refer to as *interpersonal* or *group problem solving*. This is a major part of the total managerial problem-solving process.

ASSESSING THE NATURE OF PROBLEM-SOLVING MEETINGS

Before going into the details of the methods and processes that can be used in managerial problem solving, let us focus on a model of problem analysis. Not all problems that occur at work are interpersonal in nature. For example, if a machine breaks down and you have the knowledge, skill, and resources to correct the fault and your action will be acceptable to others, then there will be no need to enter into group discussion. However, if you do not have the capacity or, indeed, are short of time, then you will have to discuss with someone else how the job is to be done and by whom.

Before proceeding further, it is important to have a way of distinguishing between those problems that require a group problem-solving approach and those that can be resolved personally.

Problem Solving in Groups

A group problem occurs when either:

1. You have a solution which is effective and acceptable to your co-workers which requires to be communicated to them and queries to be answered.

2. You do not possess sufficient information to resolve the problem personally.

3. It is necessary for others to accept and/or implement solutions which they would be reluctant to do without being involved in the problem solving discussion.

A clear example of factors 2 and 3 operating to produce an interpersonal problem situation occurs when a new production manager of a group first meets his foreman to assess work allocation. In such a situation, it is both unlikely that he would have sufficient information to make a unilateral decision, and moreover if he did take such a decision without discussion, it is doubtful that it would be properly implemented.

However, in many situations the manager may feel that he has the necessary information to solve a problem, but is aware that failure to discuss with others involved would lead to the rejection of the solution. Take, for example, the manager who is concerned with the productivity and profitability of his unit. He calculates that to buy four machines will produce a substantial saving in production costs. In particular, it will cut out the necessity for overtime and reduce the total wage bill, as well as being more efficient to operate.

In technical terms, the manager in this situation has all the knowledge required to make a decision on whether to buy four new machines. However, from an interpersonal viewpoint, he has a problem if he takes a unilateral decision. His subordinates are unlikely to accept four new machines that will cut overtime and reduce their pay. The manager's decision, therefore, is not likely to be accepted or implemented and the calculations he made on profitability and productivity will be erroneous. To effect such a change, it is necessary for the manager not only to have the technical knowledge to make a decision, but agreement and support from those implementing the decision.

Increasingly, as organizations recruit people with specialized knowledge in given professions, no one man has sufficient information and skill to make a unilateral decision. Therefore, group problem solving becomes important in terms of sharing technical information, as well as for gaining acceptance of solutions. It is for these and other reasons outlined, that business meetings are so important. Let us, therefore, look at the different kinds of meetings which can be organized, and relate them to the four case incidents with which we began.

TYPES OF MEETINGS

There are five major kinds of meetings we can consider. They are defined as follows:

A Command Meeting

A command meeting is called by the manager to instruct or direct his subordinates to undertake a specified task or establish rules governing future behaviour. The manager makes the decisions in such meetings and is accountable for the results. He decides who shall attend the meeting, what the objectives shall be, and how the work is to be achieved. The approach is therefore authoritarian, and for this form of decision-making to succeed the manager needs to have the necessary knowledge to make a high-quality decision, and a knowledge that his commands will be obeyed and implemented. This approach is characteristic of military organizations, and was characteristic of many business organizations in the nineteenth and early twentieth centuries. However, this type of meeting is decreasing in importance in business organizations for a number of reasons, such as the increase of professionals in organizations and the complexity of knowledge, high levels of employment, and the rise in democratic values. In the Robinson case described earlier, if you adopted alternative 5, deducting his pay and changing his job, then this would be an example of a command meeting.

An Advisory Meeting

An advisory meeting is called for the exchange of information. It is not a decision-making meeting. The information, once exchanged, is taken away by those involved and decisions on the next steps to be taken are made. An example of an advisory meeting might be a selection interview, where both parties ask for and receive information and at a subsequent date make a decision. An advisory meeting is therefore in essence a consultative relationship. A manager may call an advisory meeting either to inform his subordinates about ideas he has for the future, or to ask their view relating to a problem. Further examples are when a manager informs his subordinates of company plans to launch new projects, or enter new markets, or to relate matters affecting them which have come up during the manager's attendance at another meeting. Again, the manager might call an advisory meeting when he requires information from subordinates or colleagues, even though they do not necessarily need to be involved in the decision made. Likewise, subordinates can also ask for an advisory meeting to gain information which will help them either to resolve problems or to make strategic decisions.

Advisory meetings, therefore, are concerned with the sharing of facts and opinion. In reality, these meetings happen all the time, mostly on an informal basis. For example, if someone says 'Can you tell me . . .?' or 'What is your view on . . .?' or 'How can I get . . .?', then it is likely that an advisory meeting will have begun. At the more formal level, advisory meetings will take the form of consultative discussions or interviews. Alternative 3 in the Robinson case would be an advisory type of meeting.

A Collegiate Meeting

A collegiate meeting is held between people of similar status and/or professional knowledge and skill. Each person in such a meeting will have respect for the integrity of a 'professional opinion'.

Attendance at collegiate meetings is usually based upon the fact that those present have some professional knowledge or skill to contribute to the solution of a problem and implementation of the solution. Decisions in such meetings are usually made by consensus. If a person disagrees at any point, it is incumbent upon him to make clear his reasons and work toward the generation of an alternative proposition that would be acceptable to all. For example, in a meeting on the construction of a bridge, there needs to be a consensus among the engineer, the accountant, and others on the basic issues. If, for example, the accountant informed the engineer that the bridge proposed was too costly in terms of the other commitments of the company, a joint reappraisal would need to be done. It would be inappropriate in such circumstances for the engineer to ignore the accountant. It would be equally inappropriate for the accountant to disregard the engineer's opinion on the necessary resources to build a safe bridge. Accountability for decisions taken lies with the collegiate body. The collegiate meeting is becoming more important as the number of professional service advisers in companies grows. In the Robinson case, alternative 1 is likely to be a collegiate meeting where a consensus mutually agreeable solution is sought.

A Committee Meeting

A committee meeting is one in which representatives from various groups meet to make decisions on matters of mutual interest. Decisions in a committee are usually made by voting: those having the majority winning the issue. Where there is a tie, the chairman usually decides the issue by his casting vote. The committee is the traditional democratic approach to decision-making. Attendance at such meetings is usually based on one's representative role or interest in the topics being discussed. One may either represent others or oneself. Accountability for the decisions taken lies with the group rather than any particular individual, although the danger is that only those in the majority on any given issue will give support to its implementation. In the Robinson case above, alternative 4, taking the issue to the works council, would involve a committee decision.

A Negotiation Meeting

A negotiation meeting has similarities to a committee meeting, but decisions are made more on a *quid pro quo* basis, rather than voting. Each side will have different objectives but mutual interests arising from interdependence. Each side seeks to achieve the best terms, and decisions are made in relation to supply and demand factors. Decisions in such meetings are joint, and both sides are expected to support the implementation of the decision, if only to fulfil their own interests. Alternative 2 in the Robinson case provides the basis for a bargain to be developed.

CHOOSING A BUSINESS MEETING

A considerable amount of time is wasted in meetings because the members are not sure what behaviour is expected of them. A manager needs to understand what kind of meeting he wishes to hold and have an understanding that others present have a similar view. If one person comes to a meeting expecting to negotiate when the manager only wants an advisory meeting, then difficulties are likely to arise. Each side has a different expectation of the behaviour and conflict is probable.

In reality, it is unusual that one type of meeting alone is ever held at a gathering of managers. During their discussions, the nature of the meeting is likely to change. On some issues, a negotiation meeting is likely to take place. On others, people may adopt a collegiate-type meeting approach and consensus decisions may occur. In short, the nature of the meeting will change according to the issues involved.

Therefore, the task of choosing the most appropriate type of business meeting is not easy. Initially, a manager must decide whether to hold a discussion with his subordinates or co-workers. If he has all the knowledge to make an effective decision and others will accept his judgement, then it may well be that the manager can hold a command meeting, where he tells others what to do and only receives and answers questions of clarification.

To try and elucidate the decision process on managerial meetings, a flow chart has been developed (Fig. 1.1).

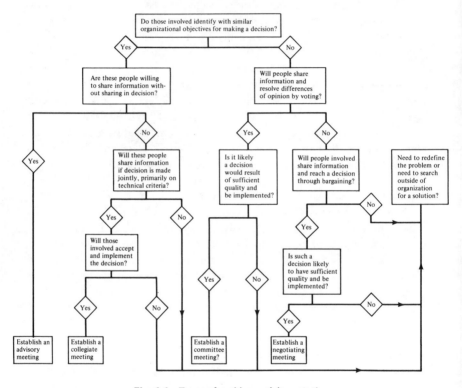

Fig. 1.1 Types of problem-solving meetings

Attendance at Meetings

It is, then, possible to establish principles by which people are invited to meetings. Given the above points, people are invited to meetings for the following reasons:

1. They want to present or share a problem.

2. They have or require information or skills appropriate to the resolution of the problem.

3. They have an interest in and influence on the extent to which any solutions will be accepted and implemented.

People can be invited to meetings for other reasons, e.g., as part of a training programme, or out of courtesy, but the above criteria define the essential and necessary basis for gaining effective decisions.

IMPLICATIONS FOR ALTERNATIVE MEETINGS

Given the above alternatives, what implications do they have for the problems of each of the managers identified earlier in this chapter? Let us, first, take the problem of the works manager who has heard that the shop stewards are planning to restrict output to gain overtime. He could examine the following alternatives:

1. Call the shop stewards together and tell them that anyone found to be deliberately restricting output will be dismissed for breach of contract.

2. Call together his twenty supervisors and put the problem to them for joint discussion and common agreement.

3. Call the shop stewards in and ask them if the information he has about restriction of output is accurate.

4. Call the shop stewards and negotiate with them an agreement regarding output and wages.

5. Establish a group of managers and shop stewards to look into the problem and produce a report on the issue.

If the manager takes alternative 1 as his major approach, he will seek to operate a command meeting. The danger he faces is that his solution will not be acceptable to the shop stewards. If they have a strong position, such as the availability of work in the area, they may well ignore the manager's threat. During the meeting, the shop stewards may also seek to change the meeting into a negotiative-type. For example, one of them might say, 'We know what the rulebook says, but that doesn't pay our bills. What we want is more money. Our claim is for a five per cent increase, and if we don't get it then we shall have to fix it through the overtime system.' Here, the manager has to make a choice. Does he enter into a negotiation or keep the meeting at the command level? If he wishes to do the latter, then he will say, 'I have not asked you here to argue about the case. The action you propose is a clear breach of an agreement. I shall take action against any man infringing it. If that is clear, then I don't think we have anything else to discuss.'

Given the industrial relations climate of today, such an approach is not likely to be effective, although during the 'thirties a similar approach often worked because of the economic problems and lack of alternative employment.

Therefore, the manager might try to establish a collegiate meeting. This is alternative 2. Here, he brings together all his immediate supervisors and seeks to work out a common policy which everyone feels able to operate. This meeting would be characterized by everyone exchanging views on the problems and contributing to a joint solution upon which all were agreed. This would then be the basis for managerial action when confronted by any moves from the shop stewards.

Alternative 3 invites the supervisors to an advisory meeting. Here, they are not invited to share in the decision process. They are only asked to give information to the manager, who reserves the right to assess and make decisions as a result.

Alternative 4 clearly calls for a negotiation meeting. The shop stewards will be asked to ensure output for an agreed wage settlement. The meeting will be held on a *quid pro quo* basis.

Finally, the manager has the alternative of setting up a committee. Each side would have representatives and the committee asked to produce a report, which at a later date might form the basis of a command or negotiation meeting.

In practice, a manager may well use one or more of these meetings to resolve the problem. The important point is where does the manager lay his priority? Does he start with a command meeting and end up having a negotiation meeting? If this occurs, is it deliberate? Does the manager feel he has lost status if he is forced to negotiate?

The dividing line between the sorts of meetings identified is not always clearcut. There are major areas of overlap in most discussions between people regarding joint problems. The distinctions made in this chapter are designed to illustrate the strategic options open to managers. However, in the actual hurly-burly of discussion it is recognized that the boundaries become blurred. Nevertheless, it is still important for a manager and those he is meeting to share a common view on what type of meeting they wish to hold.

For example, the sales manager in the second example called his salesmen together. He said, 'I would like to have a collegiate meeting. I mean by this that I would like everyone to examine the problems of our declining sales and work out a joint solution which we can all agree upon and operate.' With a statement like this, everyone in the room would have a clear expectation of what sort of a meeting the manager wanted to hold. Compare this with the research manager who called his research team together. He started by saying, 'As far as I'm concerned, this is a command meeting. We have discussed the issue of pure research for long enough. Now I'm telling everyone that from now on we only work on applied projects. I have two ideas here and these are to be started on immediately.' Clearly, everyone would know what sort of meeting this was, even though they might disagree and try to change it.

There are occasions when the manager may care not to make his preference known. He may prefer to let things develop in the meeting until such time as he perceives what he regards as the best strategy to adopt. Each person must do what he feels is appropriate to his own situation and problems.

Conclusion

This chapter has outlined the importance of managerial communication in resolving problems. In particular, attention has been focused on the nature and structure of managerial meetings. It is in such meetings that managers spend most of their working week. In the subsequent chapters, we shall identify various approaches that managers adopt in group problem-solving meetings to communicate with each other and resolve problems.

Summary
A. In this chapter, attention has been drawn to:
  - The proportion of time managers spend in group work.
  - The five major kinds of business meeting.
  - The process of choosing the appropriate business meeting.
  - The nature of problem-solving meetings.
  - The probable behaviour patterns in business meetings.
B. In particular, the chapter should enable the manager to:
  - Identify the alternative meetings available.
  - Choose a business meeting to fit the problem.
  - Recognize the need for flexible interpersonal problem-solving behaviour in given meetings.
  - Develop a strategy for conducting business meetings.
C. In considering the ideas raised in this chapter, the manager should ask himself:
  - Do the people attending my meetings know what sort of meetings they are?
  - Have these people had training in conducting various types of meeting?
  - In what way could our business meetings be improved?

2

MANAGERIAL PROBLEM-SOLVING BEHAVIOUR

Ray Taylor is a supervisor in a manufacturing plant. He has eighteen men in his department. Each Friday, he puts up the work allocation sheet for the next week. All the operatives are on piecework. The rate varies with the units being assembled. This week, three different assemblies have been assigned to Taylor's department. Taylor allocates the people whom he regards as his best workers to the high-rate, but more complex, jobs.

Within half an hour of the work allocation notice being posted, Jack Burns, aged 50, came to see Taylor. Burns had worked with the company for over thirty years. However, he was not now as quick as many of the younger members of the department. Taylor had, therefore, allocated him one of the less complex units which took less time to do but had a lower piece-rate. Burns could still earn as much as other operatives, but he had to produce a higher quota of units. He therefore came to complain to Taylor about his work allocation. 'Look,' said Burns, 'I've worked in this department longer than anyone. The rate I get paid in comparison to others has gone steadily down and now I'm on the bottom rung and have the dull jobs to do. I don't mind doing the low-paid jobs once in a while, but I'm fed up with the way I'm treated.'

Ray Taylor had a number of possible responses he could make:

1. 'This is an important order. Work on the unit I allocated you next week, do a good job, and I will make sure you get a better rate next time.'

2. 'The reason you are on the lowest rate is that your speed has fallen off. Why has this happened?'

3. 'You feel you are not being fairly treated?'

4. 'The job I've allocated to you is an important one, and I would be obliged if you would take it on. Given your age, I feel that the more easy-paced jobs are best suited to you.'

5. 'Look, I make the decisions on work allocation. I have given you the C-unit for next week. That's my decision and that's final.'

Taylor has to choose which of the five alternatives, however worded, is the most appropriate. The basis for a choice can be assessed according to the criteria of problem solving which we shall outline. There is no best answer, only answers which are either appropriate or inappropriate for the situation. Our aim, therefore, is to identify the conditions under which an informed choice can be made.

PROBLEM AND SOLUTION ORIENTATIONS

When two or more people meet to consider a problem, two approaches can be adopted. One approach involves *problem*-centred behaviour, the other *solution*-centred behaviour.

Problem-Centred Behaviour

The emphasis in problem-centred behaviour is on the search for relevant information. This in itself seems straightforward. However, research shows that giving and gaining information is a part of managerial work which managers rank as one of the most important areas of their job. It is a part which demands considerable skill.

Problem-centred behaviour has two major dimensions which we will refer to as the consultative approach and the reflective approach. The nature of these approaches will be defined later.

Solution-Centred Behaviour

The emphasis in solution-centred behaviour is on the development and advancement of ideas which are intended as possible solutions to problems. A person offering a solution, in theory at least, has diagnosed the problem and feels he has an answer that has sufficient acceptability and merit to resolve the problem. In practice, however, people often engage in solution-centred behaviour when it is inappropriate.

Solution-centred behaviour has three major dimensions. These we shall refer to as the directive, the prescriptive, and the negotiative approaches. The nature of these approaches will also be outlined, and the discussion will focus on when such behaviour is appropriate to the situation.

MANAGERIAL PROBLEM-SOLVING MODEL

Given the above distinction between problem-centred and solution-centred behaviour, the visual representation of the relationship shown in Fig. 2.1 is designed to further discussion. In particular, it illustrates the main inter-personal problem-solving approaches referred to above. When engaging in problem-solving discussions, one or more of these approaches are employed. However, at any one point of time we are either above or below the line that separates solution-centred conversation from problem-diagnostic-centred discussion. This is a vital distinction in the process of problem solving. It is important to define each of the five managerial problem solving (MPS) approaches.

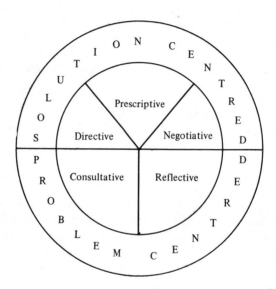

Fig. 2.1   Managerial problem-solving approaches

Directive Orientation

In some situations, where a manager has a problem involving others, the appropriate behaviour will be to take the direct line and issue an order. In effect, the manager seeks to resolve the problem by telling other people what action they must take. The directive approach of interpersonal problem solving is today most common in the armed services. An order given by a senior officer, if disobeyed, can lead to a court martial. In business, the use of the directive approach has been played down, yet it is still an appropriate form of behaviour given certain situations.

For example, an employee is caught stealing a rare piece of metal from the factory. The regulations established between the company and the unions, and accepted by employees, state that any such theft shall be punished by the termination of the offender's employment. In such a situation, the works manager would be clearly within his legal rights to terminate the man's employment.

However, if the same management were to direct an employee to work overtime when no established agreement existed on such working, then the directive would be inappropriate. When, therefore, is a directive an appropriate approach to use to resolve problems?

The directive approach is likely to be appropriate when:

- there is an accepted agreement between the parties concerned regarding the rights and duties, and authority of the manager and his employees; and/or
- both manager and his subordinates or colleagues have knowledge of the situation and recognize the need for the use of the directive approach; and/or
- the manager has diagnosed the problem and has the available knowledge to make a decision and the employees trust and accept his judgement; and/or
- time is short and those involved accept the directive approach as an expedient; and/or
- there is a highly structured task to be done, the relationship between the leader and the members is good, and the leader has positional/role authority to issue directives.

The essential characteristic of the directive MPS approach is that the manager makes the decision. An important factor in the approach, as with all the other approaches, is that the outcome should be accepted by the parties concerned and implemented to achieve an effective response to the problem.

It is, of course, in some situations possible to exercise the directive approach by a direct use of power. That is, others have to comply with the manager's wishes because they fear the consequences of disobeying. In such situations, the person issuing the directive has little concern for the acceptability of the command. He knows he can force compliance. If a manager finds himself in such a powerful situation, he must nevertheless question the effect directive action will have on his subsequent managerial selections. A directive approach is neither 'good' or 'bad' in itself.

If in the case incident outlined earlier, Taylor had chosen the fifth response, then he would have been adopting a directive response and reiterating his decision.

Prescriptive Orientation

When confronted with a problem, we often say to the person who raises the issue 'Maybe you ought to . . . .', or 'Perhaps it would be a good idea if . . . .'. These are prescriptions. The prescriptive approach to the solution of a problem really involves one person saying to another 'Try this as an answer, it might work'. All of us have used this approach. Whenever we give advice and offer suggestions, we are being prescriptive. The prescriptive approach is likely to be appropriate when:

- there is a thorough understanding of the problem presented; and/or

- the person presenting the problem has high trust and confidence in you as manager; and/or
- there is a need for as many ideas and solutions as possible to be generated; and/or
- the other person asks for your solution; and/or
- your solution will help resolve the problem.

This approach involves only making a suggestion. It is important for the manager to make sure that his subordinate recognizes it as such, and does not take it as a command. The decision lies with the recipient.

In the case incident, Taylor suggested to Burns in the fourth response that, given the latter's age, the slower-paced job was best suited to him. This was a prescriptive act.

Negotiative Orientation

In many situations, a manager recognizes that the employees will only comply with his plans if they obtain something in return. For example, men who are asked to do dirty or dangerous work are frequently promised a bonus or special payment as an inducement. The economic bargain is the most familiar instance, although many other forms of bargain are struck in work situations. Every time managers and employees make an agreement, written or verbal, an element of bargaining is involved. For example, a manager tells an employee that he requires a repair done on a machine as quickly as possible. The employee agrees to have it ready within twenty-four hours. This is regarded as a favour and part of a tacit understanding that the manager will help the employee out of a difficulty, should the occasion arise.

Bargaining is a well-established approach, influencing people's behaviour at work. All bargains imply some form of reciprocation, if not compromise. One party is prepared to give something to the other in return for something which may or may not be specified. The result is a contract, not usually written down, but understood more as a 'gentleman's agreement'.

Negotiating as a way of resolving an interpersonal problem is likely to be appropriate when:
- it is acknowledged by both parties that, whereas they have a joint interest in the solution of the problem at hand, they have different or conflicting objectives; and/or
- both parties have a relationship where they need and depend on each other for help; and/or
- both parties do not trust each other to a marked degree but are prepared to work together, provided an agreement which is mutually satisfactory can be arranged.

In the case incident, Taylor would have established a negotiative response if he had adopted the first of the alternatives in which Burns was promised a better rate next time, if he made a success of the present job.

Establishing a solution to a problem by bargaining, is a joint decision of the parties involved. The behaviour that results from this negotiation may well leave the manager with a considerable area in which to exercise his authority on such matters as task allocation, overtime, and other aspects of work involving his subordinates, but he does so within the framework of the contract established.

Consultative Orientation

A manager adopts a consultative approach when he conducts his relationships with subordinates primarily on a basis of the giving and receiving of information. A manager using this approach reserves the right to make the final decision on what should be done, but gives his subordinates the chance to ask questions, as well as answer those he presents. The consultative approach concentrates on the generation and sharing of knowledge.

When confronted, for example, with a problem concerning a dispute over a man alleged not to be doing his job properly, the manager will first question him thoroughly. The manager first tries to establish the facts, for he believes a knowledge of all aspects of the problem is vital to making a decision.

The consultative approach is most appropriate when:

- there is sufficient trust between the manager and employees that an honest sharing of information can take place; and/or
- there are common objectives by both parties in sharing the information; and/or
- one or both parties lack knowledge which is important to them and which can be obtained through consultative discussion; and/or
- both parties recognize the need for problem diagnosis through mutual questioning.

In the case described above, the second response was a consultative type of approach in which Taylor asked Burns about the reasons for his lack of speed.

The generation of knowledge through this approach may or may not produce a solution to the problem. The process of questioning may, in fact, make it clear that there is a need for a move to a directive, prescriptive, or negotiative approach. However, while at the consultative stage, it is the questioner who determines the area, range, content, and nature of the discussion.

Reflective Orientation

The distinction between the reflective and consultative orientation is subtle but crucial. When employing the reflective orientation, the manager does not seek to direct the conversation. It is the manager's job only to listen and reflect back to the other party the crucial elements of what he feels the presenter regards as the problem. The manager's task is to help the employee think through his problems so that the decision he reaches on what to do shall be his own.

In the third response in the case incident, Taylor had the opportunity of reflecting Burns's remarks about his problems. By doing this, Taylor may learn more of Burns's problems.

The reflective and listening orientation is likely to be most appropriate when:

- there is some confusion as to the exact nature of the problem expressed by the presenter of the problem; and/or
- there are strong feelings, perhaps hostility, expressed by the presenter of the problem; and/or
- the objectives of the presenter and listener may be in conflict; and/or
- the level of trust of the presenter in the receiver is not high; and/or
- there is difficulty in understanding what the presenter is seeking to communicate; and/or
- there are major issues involving each of the parties' values at stake.

These conditions will, although not necessarily all at the same time, make the listening orientation appropriate. The eventual decision can only be taken by the presenter of the problem, even if his decision means that the presenter asks for advice, direction, or some other mode of interpersonal approach from the manager.

BEHAVIOUR AND EXPECTED RESPONSES

The above five approaches to interpersonal problem solving form the basis for assessing in more detail the behaviour of people at work when confronted with problems involving other people. The points made in the analysis of the styles so far can be summarized as shown in Fig. 2.2.

MPS approach	Decision-maker	Orientation
Directive	Manager	Solution-centred
Prescriptive	Recipient	Solution-centred
Negotiative	Joint decision	Solution-centred
Consultative	Questioner	Problem-diagnostic
Reflective	Problem presenter	Problem-diagnostic

Fig. 2.2

All the time, we are by our actions making assumptions that others will respond positively to our behaviour. When we meet someone for the first time we tend to smile and hold out our right hand. It is our expectation that this behaviour will be reciprocated and are disturbed and put out if this does not happen. So it is when employing a particular approach to problem solving. If we use the inappropriate approach to the situation, the response of the other person is not likely to be what we expect.

However, if the situation is diagnosed correctly, in accordance with the principles outlined, it is possible to estimate with some accuracy the employee response. Assuming, therefore, the appropriate approach is used for a given situation, it is reasonable to expect the following reactions:

When the Manager . . .	*Employees will . . .*
• Directs	Engage in specified performance.
• Prescribes	Evaluate and/or try prescription.
• Negotiates	Establish a contract.
• Consults	Give information/ask questions.
• Reflects	Develop and think through information and feelings.

APPROACHES TO MANAGERIAL PROBLEM SOLVING

The major dimensions of managerial problem-solving behaviour can be identified by responding to a number of critical questions. These questions have been converted into a network which provides a basis for a decision on the appropriate approach to use in various situations (Fig. 2.3).

This network is more of a shorthand guide for thinking about the various approaches to use, rather than a comprehensive system for action. It serves to indicate the range of approaches and the broad conditions under which each approach should be considered.

In day to day discussion we tend to move from one approach to another, depending on our perception of the situation and the way others interact with us. We shift our approach almost intuitively. Many people, however, have a favourite approach which they seek to use whenever the opportunity presents itself. The importance of the network is that it summarizes the issues raised and provides a visual aid to enable you to assess your intuitive day to day responses within the context of the principles outlined.

It is important to emphasize that each of us uses all of the approaches outlined. Furthermore, there is no one best approach suitable to all occasions. Each interpersonal problem that emerges needs to be assessed on its merits before a particular approach is adopted. Indeed, in the resolution of any one problem it is better to adopt a number of MPS approaches as the situation changes. However, each person tends, as mentioned, to have one particular approach that he prefers to others. This preference can be measured by means of an MPS measurement index. In discovering one's personal orientation, it is possible to assess the extent to which one concentrates too heavily on a particular approach, or has a well-balanced emphasis on all approaches. In short, the approach a person uses will depend upon his personal preference, the problem he faces, his job, the time at his disposal, the attitude and power of the other party, and numerous other factors. However, it is possible to

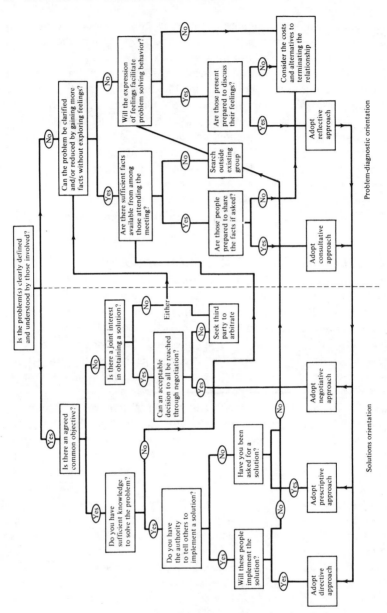

Fig. 2.3   Managerial problem-solving orientations

make a broad comparison between the main forms of behaviour expected in the meetings identified in chapter 1 (Fig. 2.4).

The matrix emphasizes the extent to which one is likely to find various interpersonal approaches in different meetings. The matrix is but a guide. If a manager sets out to have a collegiate meeting and finds there is a considerable amount of directive and negotiative behaviour, then he needs to

MPS Approaches

Type of Meeting	Directive	Prescriptive	Negotiative	Reflective	Consultative
Command	Very high	High	Low	Low	Low to moderate
Negotiative	High	Very high	Very high	Low	Moderate to high
Advisory	Low	Moderate	Low	High	Very high
Committee	Low	High	Moderate	Moderate	High
Collegiate	Low	Very high	Low	Moderate to high	High

Fig. 2.4 Probability of managerial problem-solving approaches in various meetings

reconsider the situation. Either he has initiated an inappropriate meeting to cope with the task, or those present do not have a common understanding of the objectives. It is in looking at the matrix and assessing the behaviour in meetings that a manager can begin to identify the sort of relationships that are required.

Conclusion

This chapter has distinguished between problem-centred and solution-centred behaviour. More specifically, five major forms of interpersonal problem-solving behaviour have been developed. These approaches to problem solving in group situations will be the basis for a fuller examination of managerial relations in work groups.

Summary

A. In this chapter, attention has been drawn to:
   - The five major approaches that can be used in managerial problem solving.
   - An outline definition of these five approaches, specifying the situations in which their use is most likely to be appropriate.
   - Expected responses when MPS approaches are used in appropriate situations.

B. In particular, the chapter should enable the manager to:
   - Assess the approaches he presently uses when confronted with interpersonal problems.
   - Establish a basis for developing a clear concept of which MPS approach to use in given situations.
   - Develop a deeper understanding of the factors influencing effective interpersonal communication.

C. In considering the behaviour approaches listed, a manager should ask himself:
   - Do I adopt any particular MPS behaviour pattern more frequently than others?
   - Which do I most need to improve upon?
   - How do others react when I adopt each MPS approach?

3

PROBLEM DIAGNOSIS

The five main approaches to interpersonal problem solving can be seen as emphasizing either the diagnosis of problems, or the generation of solutions. A critical fault in most people's attempts at all forms of problem solving is that they are prone to jump towards a solution before they have sufficiently understood the problem. A sound remedy must depend upon a thorough diagnosis. A pain in the chest could be indigestion, or the beginning of a heart attack! The remedies offered for these two complaints are vastly different. Likewise, the symptoms of an interpersonal problem may not indicate the real difficulty, and this requires the development of problem diagnostic skills.

Therefore, before the generation of a possible solution begins, it is important to know how to set about handling problem diagnosis. This chapter identifies some of the critical factors that need to be assessed and dealt with, if effective managerial problem solving in group situations is to be achieved.

ILLUSIONS AND REALITIES

Whenever a problem occurs, the important initial step is to gather sufficient information to allow the development of possible solutions. However, the acquisition of information is not easy. For example, imagine you are walking down a street and you see some people running from a shop. A robbery is in the process of taking place. The thieves make their getaway in a car. You feel it is your duty to inform the police what you have witnessed.

At the time of the robbery, things happened very quickly. Even so, you are convinced you got a clear view of what occurred. Other people who were about at the same time also felt they gained an accurate view of events. However, when observers are questioned there is invariably a difference in their stories. Some people allege there were three thieves, others say four. Some say the car was black, others say it was dark blue. Some say the registration began BCF, others say it was DGF. The description of the thieves also varies from observer to observer.

No one in these circumstances wishes to question the integrity of the observers, but they cannot all be correct. There is therefore a prime difficulty in problem diagnosis, simply the collecting of valid information. This is particularly difficult in situations where the issue is an interpersonal problem.

When dealing with such a situation people's feelings are liable to govern what they see and hear. All of us tend to have blinkers on. We see very often what we want to see. Take, for example, the case of an operative who is sacked for being inefficient at his job. The works manager in question has warned the operative three times about his low production record, his attitude towards the maintenance of his machine, and his persistent inclination to leave his machine unattended while he talks with other operatives. The works manager, therefore, calls in the operative and dismisses him from the company's employment.

Within one hour a strike takes place, involving all operatives in the works. They claim that the man has been unfairly dismissed, and that he has been victimized. Furthermore, they inform the works manager that they will not return until he has been reinstated.

Here is a common interpersonal problem of conflict which arouses strong feelings on both sides. Both manager and operatives consider they have solid grounds for the position they have taken. Can both sides be correct? Have they both considered all the facts? How far is their behaviour governed by their feelings, regardless of the facts? Is it possible to bring about a resolution of the problem in an ordered and time-saving manner?

The group problem-solving approach aims to enable these questions to be dealt with in a systematic manner, and thereby clear the way for a decision acceptable to both parties. This chapter outlines the initial stages of this process which must start with the separation of facts from opinions.

INFORMATION GENERATION

An initial step in the problem solving, as already stated, is to separate out facts from opinions; a difficult task, for the two are often closely mixed. To aid the process, a list should be established of things that can be considered primarily as fact and those that are beliefs.

For example, in the case of the dismissed operative, the lists would appear to *management* as follows:

Facts
- Operative did not keep up with production norms.
- Operative did not maintain machine to standard.
- Operative on occasions left his machine unattended.
- Works manager had warned operative on three previous occasions.
- Works manager dismissed man.

Beliefs

Associated with these facts, management had certain beliefs or feelings about the man in question. These were:
- He was a bad example and influence to others.
- He was a troublemaker.
- He was lazy.
- Employees on strike are irresponsible.

The facts and beliefs as seen by the *operatives* who were on strike were as follows:

Facts
- Operative had been warned three times.
- Operative left his machine unattended.
- Works manager dismissed him.
- Dismissed operative was trying to organize others into a union.

Beliefs
- Works manager was unfair.
- Works manager was looking for a scapegoat.
- This dismissal could be the beginning of many more, and an excuse for not paying redundancy payment.
- Works manager is against unions.
- Works manager is trying to become too powerful.

SHARING FACTS AND BELIEFS

In the above example, a major step to resolving the problem would be to identify and separate the facts and beliefs in a group problem-solving (GPS) meeting, where the points arising could be shared and discussed. The result in this case would be that both management and operatives would increase their knowledge of factors associated with the dispute. Information on the facts would show that the works manager dismissed the man for reasons which the employees did not know about. However, the employees could produce evidence that the dismissed man's behaviour was related to his union activities.

This sharing of information would be important in the light of the beliefs that each side in the conflict had about the other. These beliefs may or may not be correct. If they are not correct, then the danger is that each side behaves according to *assumptions* rather than *facts*. This is perhaps the single most important contributory factor to the escalation of interpersonal conflict. It is vital that all assumptions, opinions, and beliefs must be checked to see if they are based on fact.

In the above case, the dispute needs to be re-examined by both the manager and operatives. The decision of the works manager may be the same, even after this, but the new information may lead to *positive* group problem solving, where both sides recognize the need for the development of solutions that could be of mutual advantage. Once this stage is reached, there is a move towards interpersonal progress.

POSING THE PROBLEM

So far, we have been concerned with identifying the problem—separating facts and beliefs. Alongside this process, it is important to consider how an interpersonal problem is discussed. A manager in this case, for example, has a choice of posing the problem either in:

1. personal terms; or
2. situational terms.

At the meeting with the operatives, he can start the proceedings by identifying the particular behaviour adopted by the dismissed operative as the centre of the problem. In doing so he not only *personalizes* the problem, but *closes down* the area for discussion to a relatively narrow focus. The danger involved in this approach is that the personalization of the problem will evoke strong feelings in those who seek to defend their colleague. In such a dialogue, there is the likelihood that the manager and operatives will become *locked* in on one aspect of the total problem which centres on the dismissed man.

The alternative is to *open out* the discussion by a broader-based approach, in which the problem is defined in *situational* not personal terms. For example, in this case there are a number of issues which require discussing over and above whether the particular operative is dismissed. Posing the problem in a situational manner allows both parties to raise those matters they feel are important. In the present case, a situational definition of the problem could be stated by the manager in this way:

'The present difficulties that exist between us arise from a variety of causes relating to the rules governing behaviour at work, and possible misunderstandings on both sides. It is important for us all to ensure that these issues be discussed and decisions made whereby people can say they have been treated fairly. We have the opportunity here to discuss the various issues and make plans for improved relationships.'

This introductory statement does not blame either side. It does not refer to personalities, but issues. It calls for positive thinking towards fair treatment and improved relations. It seeks to identify grounds where both parties have an interest in reaching an agreement that can be of mutual benefit. In short, the problem is posed in a form which emphasizes the issues and situation rather than personalities.

SYMPTOMS OR CAUSES?

Some people will feel that the above approach is too risky. They will argue that the situational method allows the other party to raise all sorts of issues other than the particular one that sparked off the conflict. They argue that by keeping to the specific issue that generated the problem one has narrowed down the area for discussion and decision. This is undoubtedly true, but it may not aid the effective solution of the problem and may lead to a concentration of effort on to the *symptoms* rather than the *causes*.

For example, in the case discussed here it would seem that the dismissed worker may have been absent from his machine, and failed to keep up his output or maintenance work not because he was lazy, but because of his union work. Now, if the manager personalized the problem he would be in danger of discussing only the symptoms. That is, discussion would focus on the man and whether or not he broke company rules, rather than the larger and presumably more important *reasons* for his behaviour.

The statement of the problem in situational terms allows for the emergence of these larger issues. An understanding of the cause of the dismissed man's behaviour may not lead the manager to change his decision. It will, however, indicate to him clearly that the problem he should be concerned with is not an individual's laziness, but the feelings and aspirations of the employees in general for union representation, which so far has been an 'underground' activity. This fact in itself says a lot about the climate of feeling among the operatives of what is considered to be acceptable and unacceptable behaviour. This may or may not be a surprise to the manager. If he is surprised, then the problem he has to deal with is much more significant than an individual's dismissal, which is essentially only a symptom.

It is important, therefore, to pose problems so that in the problem-solving process both sides can deal with causes as well as symptoms.

ENDS AND MEANS

Many attempts at interpersonal problem solving flounder because the parties involved never establish clearly the objectives they are pursuing. Sometimes, as in negotiations, this can be deliberate. More often, it is because insufficient thought is given to areas where both parties can agree. There is a tendency to look for disagreement in problem-solving meetings.

How many times have you sat in a committee and listened to a colleague outline plans? Even though 95 per cent was in accord with the general view, the predominant focus of discussion was on the 5 per cent where people disagreed. This may seem natural. However, the result is often the defeat of the plans, simply because those discussing them fail to consider the overall objectives being pursued. By concentrating exclusively on the 5 per cent where they disagree, they fail to achieve their joint objectives.

Consider tne example of the performance interview. Jim Snell is one of your up-and-coming, bright salesmen. He has had a good year, sold more than you expected, shown initiative, and is keen to progress. However, he has recently lost an order from one of your well-established customers for promising to supply your product for a given date before checking that there were sufficient stocks. The customer was justifiably angry when you could not fulfil his order and has subsequently taken it elsewhere. This means the loss to your business of one of your largest customers.

At the performance interview, it is possible to concentrate on the 95 per cent of good things Jim Snell has done, or emphasize his one major mistake. There is a tendency in most of us to single out the weak spot for comment rather than building on the strong points. The issue is the extent to which the objectives of the exercise are clear. Is the aim to punish Jim Snell, or help him build and improve on the things he has done well?

If both parties have agreed on what the end-objective of any exercise is, attention can then be focused on the *means* for achieving that end. Again, a fundamental error in interpersonal problem solving is to start discussing *means* before a common understanding of the ends each side is aiming for can be understood. This occurs when one of the parties does not fully understand the problem, but proceeds to prescribe solutions. The means take over from the ends.

A manager may say that he has difficulty interviewing new recruits. The immediate reaction may be to suggest a training course on interviewing as the means to overcoming the problem. This, however, presumes that a manager's objective is to develop skills in this area. His reason for making the comment in the first place may have been to indicate that his objective was to cease interviewing and do other work such as laboratory research.

Conclusion

In approaching such problems, it is necessary to consider the way in which the problems are posed and tackled. In this chapter, it has been stressed that it is necessary to consider whether the emphasis in problem solving will be on:

personal considerations *or* situational considerations;

facts   *or* beliefs;

shared assumptions   *or* unshared assumptions;

causes   *or* symptoms;

ends   *or* means.

Above all, it is important to think out in advance whether you wish to pose the problem in a form that generates a *win/lose* orientation or in a manner that both sides can discuss the issues to *mutual benefit*. The win/lose point emerges when the problem can only be resolved by one side winning at the expense of the other's loss. For example, in the case of the worker who left his machine to organize a union, the way to pose the win/lose argument is to personally criticize the man for laziness. Here, his colleagues will rally to the defence of the man and a win/lose situation develops. However, by posing the problem at a situational level it is possible to discuss the issues so that both sides have something to win from the discussions, even though compromise may be incurred. The important thing is that in group problem solving the problem must always be stated so that both sides have something to gain from discussing it. A situation where one side wins totally at the expense of the other will only cause resentment by the losing group, who will seek to gain their revenge in other ways.

Summary

A. In this chapter, attention has been drawn to:
  • Separating problem diagnosis from solution generation.
  • The process of problem diagnosis.
  • Identifying the danger of building solutions on incorrectly diagnosed problems.
  • Ensuring that everyone concerned with problems has opportunity for contributing knowledge.
B. In particular, the chapter should enable the manager to:
  • Identify and separate his facts and beliefs.
  • Establish a meeting for those involved to share and correct facts and beliefs.
  • Pose the problem in situational not personal terms.
  • Separate symptoms and causes.
  • Clarify ends (objectives) before proceeding to means of implementation.
  • Identify and resolve win/lose situations.
C. In considering problem diagnosis, a manager should ask himself:
  • Are both parties trying to understand each other's viewpoint?
  • Can we establish goals which both parties can pursue?
  • Does the problem diagnosis made enable solution generation to take place?

4

DEVELOPING AND EVALUATING SOLUTIONS

Group problems arise because people:
- differ over objectives;
- are in conflict over perceptions;
- have competing roles;
- are in conflict over resources;
- possess differential authority;
- have contrasting priorities.

In everyday terms, these factors are reflected in people's personal relationships when they are:
- bargaining over a wage increase;
- arguing over the meaning of a balance sheet;
- identifying and resolving a grievance;
- discussing budget allocations;
- explaining and allocating work;
- establishing a plan of action;
- conducting appraisal interviews.

Whenever such differences occur, there is the need for someone with interpersonal problem-solving skills to help resolve the conflict. So far, we have concentrated on the importance of diagnosing the problem correctly and identifying the five major interpersonal problem-solving approaches that can be used. This chapter concentrates on the process of developing effective solutions.

THE NATURE OF AN EFFECTIVE SOLUTION

The effective solution is that which has sufficient technical quality to resolve the problem, and has the necessary minimum acceptance of those who will have to implement it.

The technical quality will depend on whether the solution meets the criteria of cost, time, reliability, efficiency, and adaptability. The acceptability criterion relates to whether those involved in implementing the decision perceive the solution as something they are prepared to invest time and energy in, that has a permissible level of risk, and which they feel confident will include personal benefit.

To reach an effective solution is, therefore, in most cases, not easy. However, it is possible by systematic means to seek solutions that will work.

DEVELOPING EFFECTIVE SOLUTIONS

Let us take a practical example, and analyse it to develop an effective solution. Tom Simpson is a manager in an electrical manufacturing factory. He has a number of people working in groups, assembling small motors for washing machines, refrigerators, and other domestic goods. A year ago, the six groups working on washing machine motors had their jobs timed by the work study engineer. The engineer wrote a report and recommended that the total task could be done quicker if the groups reorganized their work so that each person did a set individual job. This was a change from the existing system, whereby each team organized its own way of working.

During the last twelve months, output in these groups has fallen by 20 per cent. Due to retirement, two of the six work group supervisors left during the year, and a third moved to another job. Further, the turnover of staff in these groups was 24 per cent compared to an average elsewhere in the factory of 14 per cent. Absence and sickness rates were also 8 per cent higher for the washing machine motor group than the average for other groups.

A diagnosis of the problem was made. Tom Simpson discussed the problem of low output, turnover, and absence with each group and the training department conducted an attitude survey. The cause of the problem was not clear. Tom Simpson felt that the problem lay with poor supervision of the work groups. The operatives felt the problem lay with the new system of work organization.

Assuming that these two definitions of the problem were the major ones arising from the diagnosis stage, what should be done to develop an effective solution? If there is no agreement on the cause of the problem, it may be useful to look for possible solutions on which there could be agreement. This may seem illogical. However, the real test is the future working relationship, and it may be that an appropriate step is to examine solutions despite different perceptions on the cause of the problem.

Initially, it is helpful to identify what each party to the problem regards as the 'ideal situation', if the problem were to be resolved. Most people have in the back of their minds a concept, however vague, of how they would like to see the situation in the future.

Therefore, one approach is to get each party to identify its concept of the solution. This should be done by asking the individual or group to write down its views. These can then be compared with the other party's solution. Where there is similarity in the view of the ideal solution, action plans can be developed to implement the proposal.

However, where there is a distinct difference in the solutions proposed, it is important to first establish that both groups are addressing the same problem. At this stage, the development of as many joint solutions as possible should be encouraged. The principles of brainstorming, whereby all ideas are encouraged and written down prior to judgement being made upon them, should be used.

For example, the problem considered here is one where Tom Simpson and the group have different conceptions of what the cause of the problem is. Both parties, however, could be correct. It is therefore important that both views are treated similarly.

DEVELOPING SOLUTIONS: THE PROCESS
(a) Problem Statement
That discipline on the shop floor is not of sufficient standard to ensure output required.

(b) Who States Problem
Manager: Tom Simpson.

(c) Possible Solutions: The range of alternatives

Simpson	*Group*
• Hire better quality supervisors.	• Promote existing employees to supervisory positions, rather than hire outsiders.
• Train supervisors more thoroughly.	• Get rid of supervisors altogether.
• Give supervisors more authority.	
• Set employees strict targets.	• Define the supervisor's job more clearly.
• Put employees on a bonus system.	
• Make employees' job descriptions clear by writing them down.	• Give supervisors authority to give time off and decide pay rates.
• Have weekly meetings between supervisors and operatives on work.	
• Give supervisors a course in management methods.	

- Deduct pay for lateness.

- Develop stronger rules.
- Abolish overtime.

- Negotiate a bonus deal for increase in productivity.
- Establish joint consultation.

Clearly, many of these solutions are contradictory.

Rarely, is there any one answer that is going to solve a problem. The important point is to try and get as many answers from those with the knowledge and authority to implement a solution. In this case, it means Simpson and his group. Only when this has been done should judgements be made and decisions taken.

The same procedure must be gone through for each problem. For example, the operatives in this case saw the problem stemming from the new work procedure.

(a) Problem Statement
That the new work procedures are not acceptable to the employees and this has resulted in a slow down in production.

(b) Who States Problem
Employees.

(c) Solution Possibilities

Simpson
- Do work study again.
- Have a special training programme.

- Dismiss people who produce below standard.
- Test new employees for speed.
- Train operatives to measure own performance.

- Change payment system to measured day work.

Employees
- Get rid of work study system. Go back to old system of work organization.
- Give longer rest periods.

- Increase the rate for the job.

- Allow more consultation.
- Put groups on a group bonus system.

Again, the solutions are not always compatible, but there is now more information available from which to choose the solutions that could improve the situation.

THE CHOICE OF SOLUTIONS
At this point the manager is concerned with two issues:
1. What approach should he use in choosing solutions?
2. Which solutions should be chosen?

The basic issue that needs to be confronted here is which problem-solving approach should be taken. Should the manager *direct* and command the solution? Should he *prescribe* which route should be followed? Or should he bargain and *negotiate*?

The approach he will use must depend on the nature and importance of the proposed solution. If the solution proposed is central to the policy of the company, then the manager may not feel able to prescribe or bargain. He must, unless policy is under consideration for change, be directive on such issues and use his veto when he cannot agree. However, where he feels that there is little to be lost through advising and persuading, he will prescribe. Likewise, the employees will do the same in such circumstances. On solutions which involve give and take, the manager and the operatives will negotiate.

The central issue throughout can be assessed as shown in Fig. 4.1.

Solution Criteria

		Minimum Quality Level	Minimum Acceptance Level
People Involved	MANAGER		
	EMPLOYEES		

Fig. 4.1

It is vital that both parties are clear on what the levels are and the reason for establishing them.

THE PROBLEM-SOLVING MIX

The factors in the above examples identify some of the issues that need to be considered. But the context of consideration is the extent to which the problem or problems are clearly stated and the availability of solutions. The model in Fig. 4.2 identifies the dimensions of this problem-solving mix and points to some avenues of exploration from the approach developed in this book.

Approach A: Here, the problem is not clear but solutions are available. This corresponds to the case described above. The approach suggested is to

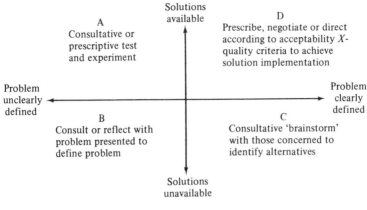

Fig. 4.2

test and experiment with the solutions to see if on an empirical basis they work and are acceptable.

Approach B: Here, the problem is not clearly defined, nor are solutions available. This requires a consultative and/or reflective approach as it is important to gather information and narrow the area for decision.

Approach C: In this instance, the problem has been clearly identified but solutions have not been advanced. This is a situation where ideas are required and brainstorming and other methods of lateral thinking need to be employed.

Approach D: In this situation, the problem has been clearly defined and solutions are available. The important thing to do is to establish how far the solutions are likely to resolve the problem and are acceptable to those having to put the decisions into operation.

In all meetings, the discussion will involve a decision as to which approach is required. This is not easy. Some people may feel they have clearly defined the problem and have solutions. Others may find themselves at the opposite end of the scale, where the problem is not clear and solutions are not available. It is in managing the relations between people who are at different stages of the problem-solving process that considerable skills of discussion leadership are required. The discussion leader or chairman will continually check to discover where the discussion has got to and seek to adapt the approach most appropriate.

Discussing Solutions

There is a tendency for most of us to become emotionally involved with both our diagnosis of a problem and the solution which we propose. This can blind us to reaching agreement and implementing a solution of benefit to both parties. It is, therefore, important to have some rules governing discussion when trying to develop solutions to interpersonal problems.

In all cases, it is important that:

- Both parties establish a mutual interest in achieving a solution.
- Both parties have the belief that they have the potential to resolve conflict.
- Solutions be discussed in terms of the outcome, rather than in terms of the person that proposed the solution.
- Solutions be weighed in terms of their effect on the total situation, rather than on one or two individuals.
- Available ideas be built on, rather than continually seek the 'perfect' solution.
- The problem and solution be seen from the other party's point of view: What do your proposals cost the other party? What do they enable him to gain?
- One's own arguments are examined as closely as the other party's.
- Win/lose situations are avoided.
- The strength of the other party's case be acknowledged.
- Feelings on the problem and situations be discussed.
- Solutions be tested in practice, rather than assume they won't work.

There is a great danger in generating and evaluating solutions, to fight for one solution at the total exclusion of the other. Argument often runs as follows:

Self	*Other*
I am right	I am right
because	because . . . .
You are wrong	You are wrong
because	because . . . .

This, in effect, is not a discussion: it is an exercise in self-justification and the denial of the other person's viewpoint. The result is that both parties talk long and hard, but nobody really listens.

The importance of developing as many solutions as possible, even if they are incompatible, is that it provides a 'basis' for examining and assessing the extent to which mutual solutions beneficial to both parties are available.

FACTORS ASSOCIATED WITH ACHIEVING SOLUTIONS

There are five main reasons why solutions may not be achieved and converted into action. Having considered the approach to generating and evaluating solutions, let us consider the problems in achieving a successful solution.

1. *Shortage of ideas* This is rarely a problem in developing solutions. Where it is a problem, it is usually because ideas are of insufficient quality, or not allowed to develop. However, by adopting the method of brainstorming, and force field analysis, whereby forces for and against the resolution of the problem are identified, it is possible to increase the flow of

solution ideas. Another way of increasing ideas is to identify critical words or phrases associated with the problem and then see what other words or phrases come to mind which relate to the original words.

Yet another approach is to develop an analogy with the original problem and see how far the principles involved in the analogy can be used to develop solutions for the real problem. It is also possible to use past experience; problems of a similar type may have occurred before, and their solutions may be of use in the present circumstances.

2. *Ideas but no decision* More usual is the case where there is an abundance of ideas, but the parties involved cannot or will not reach a decision. They become locked in, fighting for their own answer at the expense of a solution that could be achieved if they were prepared to look for areas of mutual interest. In such cases, the basic problem is that those involved have developed skills in argument, but not in group problem solving. Thus, both sides repeat their case, developing more and more reasons to prove they are 'right' and the other party 'wrong'. In this process, they get further and further away from reaching a mutually satisfactory solution.

3. *Decisions but no action* Here, a solution is reached but by one party only. That is, there is an agreement either by imposition or default. When it comes to implementing the decision, one party opts out. This is a costly way of discovering that the original solution, or the manner in which it was reached, was inappropriate. One of the reasons for the emergence of a more democratic managerial style in many industrial companies is the realization that decisions taken without consulting employees frequently lead to little cooperation at the implementation stage.

4. *Action but objectives not achieved* Here again, a decision follows, but still the objective set out is not achieved. It may be that the objective was too difficult or unforeseen difficulties emerged. However, managers recognize that action such as restrictive practice may be designed to thwart what were thought to be agreed objectives. For example, in management–union negotiations, decisions are taken regarding the operation of the plant; but there is insufficient trust between the parties. The employees, therefore, hold back on production, even though a productivity bargain has been agreed. A solution agreed round a table must therefore be followed up by more than good intentions. Basically, effective action depends upon trust and goodwill, and this can only be earned through performance over time.

5. *Objectives achieved* This is the ideal state. A problem has been identified, diagnosed, a solution discussed, implemented, and worked upon by both sides until the objective is achieved. This can only be done through the maintenance of sound interpersonal relationships, where people have learned to talk to each other openly. It will emerge where parties to the problem seek to listen to each other's point of view, develop mutual trust, and seek to work for each other's goals as well as their own. This sounds easy enough, in theory; it is more difficult in practice.

OVERCOMING INTERPERSONAL COMMUNICATION BARRIERS

If major problems are confronted in reaching a workable agreement between two parties, then it is often appropriate to ask a third party to mediate. This is often done in labour disputes. The role of the third party is a difficult one, and the parties having difficulty resolving their differences should specify clearly what they want him to do. Should the parties wish to reach a joint solution, the role of the third party should be to facilitate discussions on common issues.

One approach is to ask each party to write down:
1. What solution they want.
2. What solution they think the other side wants.
3. What they are prepared to offer.
4. What they are prepared to accept.

The third party can then bring those in difficulty to a solution together. Here he should concentrate on:
1. Feeding back to them their declared points of joint interest and agreement.
2. Facilitating constructive discussion on how to reach a mutually satisfactory agreement on outstanding issues of disagreement.

In this latter role, the third party must not seek to make decisions, but only help those seeking a solution think up new proposals, clarify existing issues, listen to each other's case, and debate the issues rather than engage in personality conflicts.

Conclusion

Throughout the solution process, the various MPS approaches should be continually examined. If you are taking the initiative, either in problem diagnosis or solution generation, consider how the other party is behaving. Does he reject your ideas or move towards acceptance? If he begins to withdraw, what causes this? If he gets aggressive, what sensitive point have you touched upon? These questions should provide clues which will enable you to identify early in discussions the likely problems. You may feel you have the best technical solution to the problem. However, if another person or group shows resistance, seek to discuss it rather than ignore it or brush it aside. If someone says, 'I don't agree with your calculations', then ask him to be more specific, rather than reiterate your figures. On the other hand, if someone says, 'I'm not convinced we are doing the right thing by going ahead on this project', then reflect back his feelings of concern to him. For example, say 'You feel we are on the wrong track?' This gives the other person an opportunity to put his point.

The solution development and evaluation process continually must be open to reassessment, where either:
1. the technical quality of the solution is in doubt; or
2. the acceptability of the solution is being questioned.

Where, however, those involved in the meeting are satisfied that these factors are being dealt with, it is appropriate to make decisions and move on to the stage of implementation.

Summary

A. In this chapter, attention has been drawn to the importance of developing and evaluating solutions, which involves:
- Identifying the nature of an effective solution.
- Developing a range of alternative solutions.
- Establishing the criteria for solution choice.
- Recognizing the barriers to solutions.
- Interpersonal relations in solution development.

B. In particular, the chapter should enable the manager to:
- Assess the basis for developing solutions.
- Develop a method of solution development.
- Establish decision criteria for solution choice.
- Diagnose barriers to the development and implementation of solutions.

C. In considering the issues raised, a manager should ask himself:
- How do I approach the development and evaluation of solutions at present?
- Does everyone concerned with the quality and acceptability of solutions get invited to meetings?
- What happens to decisions on solutions?
- What do I need to do to improve my effectiveness in this area?

5

SOLUTION STRATEGIES

One of the major difficulties in problem solving is the presentation of solutions. Very often we refer to 'selling a solution'. This means we have to persuade and influence people, and we shall concentrate on these strategies in this chapter.

This is a field in which salesmen and advertisers have spent much time and creative energy. Their approaches, however, only build upon the various persuasion strategies that people use every day. The difference is that individuals tend to operate on a narrower range than the media-merchants. Professional salesmen not only adopt a wide range of strategies, they reinforce their message through pictures and samples, whereas the individual in a business meeting usually operates at the verbal level of expression.

We shall examine some of the major verbal strategies and tactics that people use in meetings to put forward their solutions. The three solution-orientated approaches identified earlier provide a basis for analysing these strategies. The other dimensions we shall use are the extent to which those speaking emphasize the past, present, or future.

The model in Fig. 5.1 outlines some of the major strategies that can be identified, given the perspective just mentioned.

Using the model as a reference point, we can now examine various solution presentation strategies. None of these strategies is 'right' or 'wrong'. They are only more or less appropriate or inappropriate to the situation and the people involved.

Time Focus

	PAST	PRESENT	FUTURE
Prescriptive	Precedent	Comparative	Logic
Negotiative	Obligation	Participative	Prestige
Directive	Precedent	Dictative	Predictive

Behavioural approach (row label spanning the three rows)

Fig. 5.1   Matrix identifying the alternative solution/presentation strategies:
the context of time and behaviour approach

First, let us examine these strategies in the context of given problems. A group of managers are meeting to decide whether to use the existing machinery or change to new machines. During the discussion, a manager refers to the traditional approach of not replacing machines until it is essential.

1. *Precedent*
'We have always done it that way in the past and it has worked.' Here, the man with the solution puts an historical argument. He refers people to the approach previously used successfully, and implies that this is still appropriate. This solution strategy relies heavily on precedent. Certainly, there is a clear basis for making a technical decision. Others, however, may argue that the situation has changed and argue as follows.

2. *Comparison*
'Look we are faced by competition. All our rivals have the new machines and they can produce more. I think we should buy them.'
This, again, is a technical solution strategy. The executive uses the comparative approach in which he draws attention to the factual situation. He emphasizes the situation that prevails. While his opponents would have difficulty in faulting his comparison, they may disagree with his solution. One manager points out that 'the firms with the new machines have spent a lot of money, and I think they will not be able to use the new machines due to labour disputes following the redundancies declared'. Another manager, in favour of the new machines, enters with a new persuasion strategy.

3. *Logic*
'Now these new machines have been invented, I think it is only a matter of time before they become accepted. Our machines are getting more and

more out of date and we will have to change sometime. Given that demand for our product is increasing and we have cash in the bank, I think we should interest ourselves in the new machines as the industry is going to be more competitive.'

This person examines the current situation in the company and makes what he feels are logical inferences regarding future developments. He is primarily looking to the future on the basis of present knowledge. He, therefore, concentrates on known technological facts and argues a case for buying the new machines. Again, his colleagues would have difficulty denying his facts, assuming they were accurate. They may well, however, differ on his logical deductions.

In all the above situations, the doubts expressed were not about the technical nature of the new machines, but their acceptability for various reasons. Let us imagine some of the solution strategies that might be employed to deal with this problem. For example, assuming that the group decide to buy the new machines, how do they persuade the employees to accept them? Initially, consider the approach the general manager might use when talking with the union representatives using a negotiative approach.

4. *Obligation*

'We have decided to go ahead and buy the new machines we have been considering. You will remember that we mentioned this when we negotiated the productivity bargain with you last year. At that time you agreed for a phased redundancy programme, should it become necessary, provided your members received a proportion of the increased value brought by the new machines. We are now concerned to put these ideas into effect and wish to take up our previous agreement.'

Here, the emphasis is on the past, but concentrates heavily on the acceptability of a previously agreed plan. This solution strategy is built on the concept of goodwill and a negotiated settlement. The presentation emphasizes the obligation employees have to management. A different approach would be as follows.

5. *Participation*

'The management have been considering buying some new machines which all our competitors possess. The acquisition of these new machines will cause some manning problems. We would therefore like to get together with union representatives before buying the machines, so that you have the chance to participate in decisions affecting all operatives.'

This approach does not propose a direct, but rather an indirect, solution. The emphasis is put upon joint discussion on the assumption that this will lead to a high level of acceptability for the emerging decisions. If management wished to take another approach, it could do so as follows.

6. *Prestige*

'It is important that we maintain our position as the leader in the field. Therefore, I propose we invest in the new machines, and offer the men incentives.'
Here, the proposer is concerned primarily about the future image of the company and quality of the product. He emphasizes the importance of maintaining leadership and the prestige to be gained.

Finally, in this analysis, let us look at the directive approaches that can be used, emphasizing different time perspectives.

7. *Precedent*

'It's always been done in the same way and I'm not going to change things.'

8. *Command*

In contrast, someone concerned about the here and now might respond by saying, 'I'm making the decisions on this one. We are buying the new machines, and the matter is now closed.'

9. *Prediction*

'The managers have considered the future needs of the company and have decided to buy new machines. This will have an effect on manning schedules and we have drawn up plans for redundancy. These will come into operation next month and a notice outlining them will be put up after this meeting.'
This approach indicates that decisions affecting the future have been taken and are about to be put into effect. Implicit in the approach, is a prediction that the technical quality and acceptability of the decisions are sufficient to ensure that the required action is achieved. The tone of the approach is directive and it is assumed that the managers have confidence in both their knowledge of the situation and the likely response of the people.

Some Additional Approaches

The above are but a few of the major solution presentation strategies adopted in group problem-solving meetings. Four more approaches can be defined briefly here:

1. *Analogy*

'This situation is similar to that of America when the Russians sent up their sputnik. If we don't compete, then we shall lose.'

2. *Praise*

'I think the production department has done a first-class job and the time has come to recognize that by investing this money in new machines.'

3. *Threat*
'Look, unless I get these new machines, I will have no alternative but to hand in my resignation, and that means my senior staff will leave also.'

4. *Friendship*
'We have always settled our differences peacefully and in a friendly way. Rather than upset Joe and his colleagues in production, I suggest that we go along with his proposal for new machines.'

TACTICS OF PERSUASION

The tactics of persuasion in business meetings could be a study in themselves. This would include reasons given for doing things, as well as those for preventing things from being done. We shall summarize some of these factors, although the range and diversity of the tactics will not be dealt with in depth.

Reasons Why We Should . . . .
The Good Old Days   Here, the speaker argues for the proposition on the basis of criteria pertaining to a different time and situation: 'It worked when profits were at an all time high.'

The Rising Sun   Here, the tactic is to emphasize trying something new: 'We must not bury our heads in the sand but look forward and try new ideas.'

Generalities   This tactic is often known as the 'truth-and-justice' approach. The speaker talks in generalities with references to increasing productivity, pay, and profits, and other things that people will tend to agree with, but rarely touches on the specifics of how to do it.

Transfer   'It worked in the company down the road and I think it will work here' is an example of the transfer persuasion tactic.

Selective Facts   'I think we ought to do it, because the facts show . . . .' The facts, however, have been carefully chosen to emphasize the solution the speaker wishes to be chosen.

Reasons Why We Should Not . . . .
Eric Webster* has summarized the tactics for overcoming solutions that you do not like. He calls it the 'power of negative thinking'. His list, translated into the sort of things people say in group problem-solving meetings when they dislike a particular solution, would sound as follows:

    1. 'We haven't got time to deal with that issue.'
    2. 'You are not putting that idea forward seriously, are you?'
    3. 'That's a fine idea but too advanced for our operation.'

---

* *How To Win The Business Battle*, Penguin, 1967.

4. 'But what you are saying is not new.'
5. 'The cost of this will be tremendous.'
6. 'Your idea is not in line with current policy.'
7. 'We tried ideas like this before and they didn't work.'
8. 'It sounds easy in theory but it's not easy in practice.'
9. 'A better idea is . . . .'
10. 'It won't work because . . . .'
11. 'If we could amend the idea to . . . .'
12. 'This looks like the sort of thing suggested by old Smithers just before he was sacked.'
13. 'I don't like the bit where you say . . . .'
14. 'This is typical of the sort of thing that people from your department come up with.'
15. 'I think this idea would fall foul of factory regulations.'
16. 'These new machines would cause labour problems.'
17. 'Let's adjourn and consider it later.'
18. 'Let us set up a working party on it, and get a written report.'
19. 'Yes, this idea is OK, but it could be improved if we wait a while.'
20. 'Let's wait and see what our competitors do.'

These are all tried and tested ways of deflating solutions. Indeed, most managers are intuitive experts at proposing and countering solutions. This chapter is in itself nothing new, but a reflection of the behaviour generated in group discussions. In essence, a lot of energy is used in negating ideas, rather than devising ways of producing creative group problem solving.

SOLUTION DECISIONS AND ACTION

The strategy and tactics required to ensure solutions result in action is complex. The model in Fig. 5.2 identifies the factors which determine the fate of solution ideas.

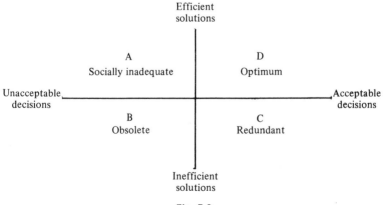

Fig. 5.2

As previously stressed, solutions to be effective must possess the power to resolve problems and be acceptable to those implementing them. The above model provides one way of looking at this situation.

A. Socially Inadequate Solutions

These are solutions that are attempted and fail because they offend the social and behavioural susceptibilities of people. Technically, the solution would work, but people do not like it for other reasons. A current example concerns high-rise blocks of flats. As a technical means of resolving a housing shortage, they are an efficient solution, judged by economic land use criteria. However, for social reasons, such as cramped facilities, lack of private play areas and gardens, and inconvenience, there have been moves to stop such development.

In business organization, many similar situations occur. Many jobs have to be de-skilled to a point where a man is but an appendage to a machine. Increased automation may be an efficient answer technically to standardizing production, but increasingly it is becoming socially unacceptable. There is a move by employees to demand work in which they can have some interest rather than be victims of an efficient technical solution.

B. Obsolete Solutions

These are solutions which are neither efficient nor acceptable. If, for example, a company wished to increase its sales, a solution might be for all the salesmen to work sixteen hours a day to cover all shops in the country. On examination, however, this solution would be inefficient as 80 per cent of sales volume comes from 20 per cent of the shops. The solution would not only be uneconomic, but socially unacceptable to the salesmen.

C. Redundant Solutions

These solutions are acceptable but inefficient. For example, if it were suggested that employees received treble pay for overtime in order to meet a production target, it would be likely to be acceptable but not necessarily efficient. However, the overtime solution would be sound if an economic trade-off suitable to both sides could be arranged. Should this be so, then the solution would become optimum.

D. Optimum Solutions

These solutions possess necessary acceptability and technical efficiency. We are continually searching for optimum solutions. They are, however, in scarce supply. The strategies outlined earlier are only ways of persuading others to accept a solution which in some way approximates to your conception of what is the optimum. But others are likely to hold different views. The result is often a compromise, somewhere within the area labelled D in Fig. 5.2.

Recognizing Solution Inadequacy

The important point in the consideration of these solutions is to recognize why any given solution is not working, or is likely to work. Is it because of a social factor? Or is it that the solution is technically inadequate? Only by identifying whether it is one of these or a combination of both, is it likely that an improvement in the managerial problem-solving process will be achieved.

Conclusion

This chapter has focused on factors which aid or hinder solutions, and has concentrated particularly on the presentation of solutions. The arguments that are advanced are based on historic, present, or future considerations and can be presented in many different ways.

The power of negative thinking is strong, and many approaches have been identified by which people try to reject others' solutions. The methods and tactics used in solution advancement and rejection can therefore be seen as a social game.

For the manager in a meeting, however, confrontation by such approaches may be highly frustrating. Why do people act 'negatively' to your 'positive' solutions? At the end of the chapter, a model was put forward which identifies in broad terms how others might view solutions. Arguments for and against may be of little effect, if others see the solution as socially unacceptable, obsolete, or redundant. In such cases, it is probable that the solution needs changing, if any effective action is to emerge.

Summary

A. In this chapter, attention has been drawn to the nature of solution strategies which involve:
   - Recognizing the time dimension in the proposal.
   - The interpersonal solution approach used.
   - The words used.
   - The implications of the solution.
   - The reception of the solution.
B. In particular, the chapter should enable the manager to:
   - Choose a way of presenting solutions.
   - Recognize the nature of opposition.
   - Identify the area in which solutions are rejected.
   - Develop solution strategies that cope with technical and/or behavioural factors.
C. In considering the issues raised, a manager should ask himself:
   - What solution strategies and tactics do I use?
   - Which are most successful and which least successful?
   - What possible changes could I experiment with in this area?

6

PROBLEM SOLVING AND MANAGERIAL ACTION

PROBLEMS, SOLUTIONS, AND ACTIONS (PSA)

So far, the discussion has concentrated on problem diagnosis and solution development. Without action, however, problem diagnosis and solution development will be wasted. The relationship between problem diagnosis, solution development, and action implementation is complex. A person can be effective as a diagnostician, but not necessarily competent in the areas of solution development or implementation.

For example, Sir Alexander Fleming discovered penicillin in 1929. However, nine years passed before the major practical application of his work was discovered by the scientists Florey and Chain. They noted a small paragraph in Fleming's work, which suggested penicillin could kill bacteria and was non-toxic. Fleming had made a thorough diagnosis of the scientific problem before him, but had only gone a small way in seeing how his work could be used to solve problems of ill-health. It was left to others to develop such solutions and foster action for the mass production of the drug which we now take for granted.

Other examples of the separation of problem diagnosis, solution development, and action implementation abound in science. In the year 1821, Faraday diagnosed the workings of the electric motor and developed a model of it. However, for more than fifty years no one extended Faraday's solution into an action programme for producing and using electric motors.

WHERE ARE YOUR STRENGTHS?

Given that there are three major strands to the problem-solving action process, it is important to know where your abilities lie. It is possible as the models in Fig. 6.1 indicate to have different problem-solving action profiles for different people. Let us, therefore, consider the characteristics of people who could have such profiles as those shown.

1. The Problem Diagnostician

The major strength of the problem diagnostician (Fig. 6.1a) is his ability to ask key questions about the cause of a problem, and to follow this up by gathering relevant information. He is usually sound at establishing objectives and an expert in using research tools. He is capable of distinguishing valid and invalid data, and assessing its reliability.

His interest is in the past. He wants to know what happened, when, where, and how it occurred. The problem diagnostician is essentially an

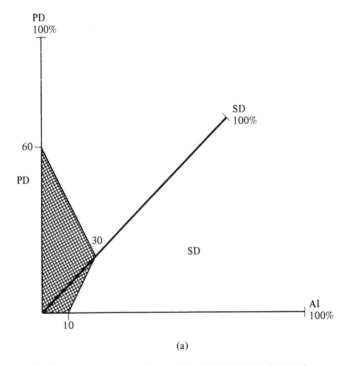

(a)

Fig. 6.1 (a)   Problem-solving action profile: Problem Diagnosis

analyst, and may even say that he has no interest in developing solutions or taking action on his findings. He feels his is a task of pure scientific discovery. However, all problem diagnosticians have a certain, if less pronounced, orientation on the other problem-solving action indices.

2. The Solution Developer

The focus of the solution developer (Fig. 6.1b) is on the future. He has important skills in taking a given diagnosis, or set of data relating to a problem, and seeing the ways such information could be used. His major strength will be in the identification of alternative lines of action.

The solution developer is a creative person who does not think necessarily in a sequential, logical, or methodical manner. He will resort from time to time to analogies, metaphors, and similes to put words to his ideas. His flights of fantasy may seem somewhat unnatural and a bit 'way out' at times. Yet, the person who first took the diagnosis of bird flight and developed the solution that men could fly by building metal wings on to a structure with an engine attached was regarded as only half-sane. The solution developer

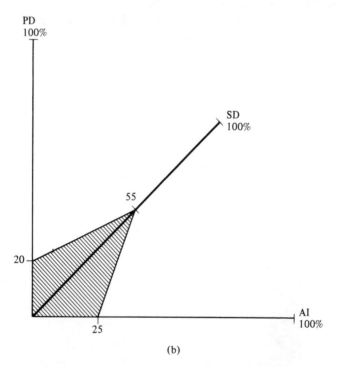

(b)

Fig. 6.1 (b)   Problem-solving action profile : Solution Development

will be concerned with anticipating events and situations with possible answers. A major strength will be his ability in envisaging a range of probable developments and putting forward contingency plans for each one.

He will be good at thinking up ideas, and building on those suggested by others. This dual process is a vital factor in effective solution development. He will tend to have an outward-looking, divergent, panoramic perspective in which numerous avenues are explored and associations examined.

The solution developer may not be effective as a problem diagnostician, nor as an action implementer. His chief value may be his visions and projections which will require the skill of others to crystallize them into action.

3. The Action Implementer

The action implementer (Fig. 6.1c) concentrates on what has to be done. Given that information on a problem has been gathered and a number of solutions developed, then the action implementer will concern himself with practical applications. His emphasis is on current needs and resources. He will be substantially concerned with how to organize people and how to achieve given objectives. He sets standards of time and cost, and manages both people and things to achieve the set goals. He is an administrator with some facets of the entrepreneur.

The action implementer is not primarily concerned with looking at causes, or the range of alternatives. His emphasis is on implementing a

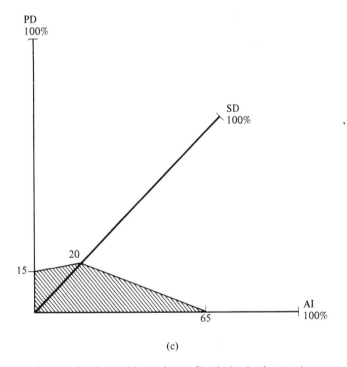

(c)

Fig. 6.1 (c)   Problem-solving action profile: Action Implementation

particular solution and assessing the consequences. This, clearly, means that from time to time he will need to exercise problem diagnostic skills if things go wrong, or become a solution developer if the existing approach needs modifying. Primarily, though, he is concerned with doing. He is an end-result man, in so far as his object is to complete a chain of events. The action implementer converts information and ideas into tangible products. He is a risk-taker who is looking for the achievement he regards as success through change.

THE PSA CYCLE

The difficulty with distinctions such as those outlined above is that they are not airtight. Clearly, every thought process can be defined as action and vice versa. It is, therefore, recognized that the distinctions are not perceived by everyone in the same way. What is problem diagnosis for one man may be action implementation as seen by another.

For example, take the case of Jim Brown, the managing director of Top Textiles. His own training had been in engineering. When he succeeded to the senior position in the family firm, he was conscious of the lack of a clear approach to marketing the products of his company. The company had a number of salesmen, but little in the way of marketing information. He therefore called in a marketing consultancy firm to (a) assess the marketing problems and opportunities of his company and (b) propose ideas on how to become more marketing orientated.

In this way, Brown contracted out the task of problem diagnosis and solution development to those with specific expertise and experience in such matters. He did not himself abdicate from such functions. Indeed, he read widely on the subject and developed some new ideas on the reorganization of sales. Even so, he saw his major task as assessing the report produced by the consultants, making decisions upon it, and then implementing those ideas he felt were appropriate to his company. He clearly felt that in this matter his skills lay in the action implementation area, not the areas of problem diagnosis or solution development.

Now, the writing of their report by the consultants constituted, to them, action, even though to Brown it constituted only part of the diagnosis and solution development. Therefore, diagnosis, solution development, and action implementation are relative phenomena related to the people and their task. If we see it as a continuum, then it looks like the model shown in Fig. 6.2.

This is a broad identification of how events can be seen to be pre-dominantly either problem-, solution-, or action-centred. No event is totally problem-, solution-, or action-centred. It is a question of which has the most emphasis at a given time.

Furthermore, the pattern is not easily identifiable. It does not always go from problem diagnosis to solution development to action implementation in clear identifiable stages. It is a mark of the effective manager that he can move with ease and flexibility among all three stages. He is quick to see the need to move from problem diagnosis, to solution development, and then into action. He is equally quick to see the need to reverse the process when

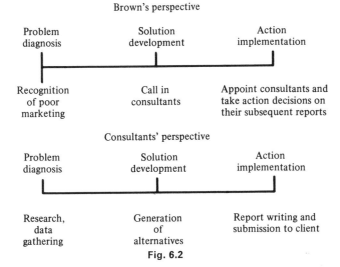

Fig. 6.2

things are not going as planned. He may not have the ability to be a good diagnostician himself, but he knows when to be diagnostic and who to call upon.

In each incident, there is a recurring process going on, as outlined in the model shown in Fig. 6.3.

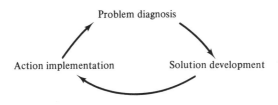

Fig. 6.3 The PSA cycle

Problem solving can fail if different people are at different stages of the cycle. If, for example, in a meeting one person keeps saying, 'I think we need more information', he is one stage behind the solution developer who is saying, 'I think we ought to accept that we have enough data and start considering the alternative answers'. Likewise, the meeting can fail if it does not accord to those people with special skills in these three areas the opportunity to exercise them.

What Sort of People?
The suggestion is that most of us have one or more preferences for problem diagnosis, solution development, or action implementation. If this is true,

how do you recognize what sort of major orientation you have and, equally important, what sort of a person your subordinate, colleague, or new recruit is?

1. Problem diagnosticians will frequently be heard to use such phrases and sayings as:

'We need more information . . . .'

'The questions that require answering are . . . .'

'Before doing anything, let's assess where we are . . . .'

'How do you feel about this . . . ?'

'When did the trouble begin . . . ?'

2. Solution developers will frequently be heard to use such phrases and sayings as:

'I think the way to approach it is . . . .'

'An alternative to that is . . . .'

'Have you tried . . . ?'

'Why don't you . . . ?'

'In my experience, it is useful to . . . .'

3. Action implementers will frequently be heard to use such phrases and sayings as:

'Let's do it now . . . .'

'John, you do the left side, I will do the other.'

'There is little risk, so let's have a go.'

'Sign here . . . .'

'Let me have our usual order by next Tuesday.'

It is harder to put forward words which express the approach of the action implementer than it is for the diagnostician or solution developer. This is reflected in the old saying that 'actions speak louder than words'. While this generalization is not necessarily true, it does reflect a basic difference in the emphasis between action implementation and the other aspects of the problem-solving action process. Actions, such as driving a car, adding up figures, drawing a plan, even writing a report, are usually done without speaking. One tends to speak with others when a problem arises, such as a broken car engine, inadequate figures, unclear specifications in a plan, and the lack of information to compile a report.

What Sort of Job?

The PSA approach you use, however, is likely to be a function of the job you are performing. Given the caveats made earlier about the relative nature of each of the categories, and the fact that we are all diagnosticians, solution developers, or action implementers at varying times, what conclusions can be drawn? Consider your own job in the context of the issues outlined below. Here, the three approaches are outlined in terms of various behaviours. It may be possible for you to estimate from the chart in Fig. 6.4 the major skills of PSA behaviour required in your job:

Problem diagnostic	Solution development	Action implementation
I ask	I suggest	I tell
I reflect	I offer	I decide
I listen	I recommend	I reward
I inquire	I advise	I judge
I inform	I warn	I refuse
I research	I propose	I allocate
I gather	I develop	I enforce
		I apply

Fig. 6.4

PSA IN PRACTICE

The diagnostic approach emphasizes a research orientation. The solution development approach emphasizes the creation of ideas to resolve problems. The action approach emphasizes the implementation of solution ideas. These ideas are represented in the model in Fig. 6.5. The model presents a summary of some of the major issues that people are likely to deal with when operating at various levels.

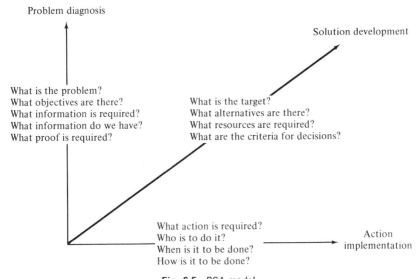

Fig. 6.5 PSA model

Planning the Work

If we accept the PSA model in Fig. 6.5 as a basis for planning work, then it is possible to develop the matrix in Fig. 6.6 within which to assess given tasks.

	Task definition	Time schedule	People involved	Resources required	Methods to be used	Location of operation
PROBLEM DIAGNOSIS	1	2	3	4	5	6
SOLUTION DEVELOPMENT	7	8	9	10	11	12
ACTION IMPLEMENTATION	13	14	15	16	17	18

Fig. 6.6 PSA work assessment plan

This assessment plan provides a basis for:

1. Asking the essential questions to complete a work task.

2. Identifying the stages which have been covered and at which blockages occur.

Let us use the model to examine a particular case through the eighteen stages outlined in the matrix.

Tom Scholes is a manager in a chemical plant. An essential part of his job is to ensure that the quality of the product is maintained. A breakdown on one of the machines made him suspicious that the composition of the product may have been affected. He, therefore, decided to look into the matter. Using the PSA work assessment plan as a means for identifying his approach, he adopted the following schedule:

1. Task definition: to discover if the composition of the product has been affected by the machine breakdown.

2. Time schedule: establish a deadline of one hour to gather information.

3. People involved: research chemists.

4. Resources required: laboratory equipment.

5. Method: chemical tests on the product.

6. Location: laboratory.

Scholes found from his tests that the product had been affected. Therefore he started on the solution development phase:

7. Task definition: to prevent such contamination in the future.

8. Time schedule: to start immediately.

9. People involved: personal subordinates and laboratory personnel.

10. Resources required: inspection equipment.

11. Methods: chemical tests.

12. Location: on site or laboratory.

Scholes held a meeting and discussed these ideas with his personal subordinates. During the meeting, they suggested other solutions, such as acquiring new machinery and establishing a gauge to show the chemical composition being put together. Scholes agreed with his men what action should be taken, and then took steps to implement the decision:

13. Task definition: to establish a chemical gauge on the machines and test twice each shift on the composition of the product.

14. Time schedule: the new process to be established within one week.

15. People involved: personal subordinates and engineering department.

16. Resources required: a gauge to measure chemical composition of product.

17. Methods: engineering followed by personal supervision of the new method of operation.

18. Location: on site.

Conclusion

This chapter has tried to identify the relationship of problem diagnosis, solution development, and action implementation. It has further suggested that most people have a certain preference and/or ability in one of these areas greater than in the others. While it is difficult to separate out the elements in any event, the chapter has pointed to the orientation that people adopt in given situations.

The issue is one of weight and balance. Everyone engages in problem diagnosis, solution development, and action implementation. The important thing is to know which of these we do best, and how far our skills are used in the problem-solving process. These issues will be considered further in looking at the conduct of business meetings.

Summary

A. In this chapter, attention has been drawn to:
- The relationship between problem solving and managerial action.
- Problem-solving action profiles.
- The delay between problem solving and action.

B. In particular, the chapter should enable the manager to:
- Identify his own problem-solving and action orientations.
- Consider in which areas most of his work falls.
- Assess the balance he wishes in a job.

C. In considering the material in this chapter, a manager should ask himself:
- Do I need to establish a different balance between my problem diagnostic, solution development, and action implementation orientation?
- How far do my problem-solving and action orientations fit the job I have?
- What should I do to become more effective in the problem-solving and action areas?

7

MESSAGES AND RESPONSES

What effect do your words have on other people in a meeting? Do they understand what you say? How far do you understand other people's words and meaning? These are central issues in all meetings.

So far, we have concentrated on the alternative types of meeting, the interpersonal approaches that can be used in group problem-solving and PSA profiles. The time has now come to concentrate on the words people use when communicating with each other. Whenever we speak to someone, it will have some effect. But is it the effect we wanted? This and succeeding chapters will examine some of the possible results of certain behaviour.

Our reaction to others depends upon a host of factors, including such things as their tone of voice, their dress, mannerisms, and so on. A major factor, however, is the words and phrases that one person uses in conversation with another. This chapter concentrates on the messages and responses that are transacted between people at work.

WORDS AND MEANINGS

Words do not always mean what they say. The reason is that we as the sender of a message do not know exactly what meaning is attached to our communication by the receiver. We look to his verbal and non-verbal behaviour to gain some confirmation that our message is received and understood as we intended it.

However, it is often the case that we are not aware of the impact that we have on others until it is too late. We may, for example, not wish to offend someone but do so accidentally. On other occasions, we may seek to bring about an improvement, say, in the work performance of others, yet we find that our words have the reverse effect of what we had intended.

For example, consider the case of Jim Walsh, works manager of an engineering company. He decided to conduct a performance review with one of his departmental supervisors. His aim was to discover how the man felt about his job, and give him help wherever possible. The supervisor, Ray Stevens, arrived for the interview which began as follows:

WALSH: Hullo, Ray, I've asked you in to discuss how your job is going on and to give help where possible. What are your feelings about the job?

STEVENS: I'm quite pleased, actually. We've got a few small problems which I'm working on but things are going well. During the last six months, we've expanded production 5 per cent with the same labour force, we improved our reject rate by 2 per cent, and absenteeism and lateness has started to go down. I could do with two more men to do jobs like stacking the units and keeping the shop clean. I think this would take the load off the skilled men on the machines and they would have more time to produce. I'm sure it would enable them to reduce their scrap-rate, too.

WALSH: Yes, that scrap-rate in your department needs looking at. It's twice as high as any other department. I know your lads produce more, but at a cost. I know you've done well on a number of things, but you must watch your scrap-rate with the cost of raw material being so high.

STEVENS: Don't forget that my department has all the old machines. All the others have some of these new 1600 type. They make a big difference to the scrap-rate.

WALSH: I know who has got what. The point is that I think improvement could be made, even with the old machines. Have you tried having a word with the men?

STEVENS: It's not as easy as that. The basic problem is that the old machines don't enable a highly efficient process. If we had a couple of extra people, however, the craftsmen could spend more time looking after the scrap problem without losing output.

WALSH: We can't take on any more labour just yet.

THE DIRECTION OF CONVERSATION

The above is an example of conversation that happens on various subjects every day. The works manager, in this case, is getting into difficulties. Let us examine what is happening. Initially, the manager sets out to discover how Stevens feels about the job and, secondly, to help him where possible.

At the beginning of the conversation, the supervisor, Stevens, is forthcoming and speaks with pride about the achievements of his department. He even points to a problem area, that of the scrap-rate. Walsh immediately seizes on this area of admitted weakness. He begins to put pressure on the supervisor rather than discuss the problem. Walsh ignores the good points and talks in a critical fashion about the weak areas. This is not untypical. In numerous real-life and training situations, this pattern has been evident. Given that 95 per cent of things are working well and 5 per cent not so well, the superior adopts a critical attitude on the small area of inadequacy.

Walsh's response leads to Stevens becoming defensive. The supervisor, in effect, stops coming forward and begins to erect explanations, excuses, and protective barriers. Up to this point, Stevens has not mentioned the fact that he is concerned about his having no new machines. Indeed, he was proud of his achievements with the old ones.

The seeds of argument have been sown. The alternative, that of a problem-solving discussion, has begun to recede. The language used by Walsh has, in effect, stopped Stevens from thinking in a positive fashion. Walsh has closed the conversation down to a small area, rather than opening it up.

Walsh should question what he is trying to achieve. If he really wants to know what Stevens thinks and to help him, then he should start asking questions or reflecting back to Stevens the points the supervisor has made. For example, when Stevens mentioned the scrap-rate problem, Walsh could have said 'Tell me more about this problem', or 'You feel that having more men would help with the scrap-rate problem?'. Either of these responses would have been an invitation for Stevens to come forward.

Win/lose Discussions

As it is, Walsh is seen by Stevens to attack and the supervisor's response is to defend. The result is that Walsh starts what could be a win/lose situation. He begins to pressurize Stevens into taking action. Walsh prescribes to Stevens that he should talk with his men. The supervisor rejects this proposal and comes back with his solution of employing more men.

At this point, Walsh will find it increasingly difficult to back down from his point, if Stevens continues to refuse. In this case, Walsh will 'lose' a point and Stevens will 'win' a point. Should this occur, Walsh, as works manager, may well feel he has lost status in the eyes of his subordinate. He may, therefore, hold out for a 'win', in which case Stevens will 'lose'. Is it necessary to get into a 'win/lose' situation like this in such discussions? The following analysis seeks to provide some guidelines or cues which can serve as indicators of how others respond to your communications and to show if you are heading for a 'win/lose' situation.

CONVERSATIONAL RESPONSES

The above conversation between Walsh and Stevens illustrates some aspects of the responses people make during conversation. For the purpose of analysis, we shall define the major responses that people will make under the following categories:

Aggressive	—	attack
Defensive	—	defend
Regressive	—	withdraw
Fixative	—	repeat
Supportive	—	help or develop.

The assumption is that whenever you make a remark to another person, he or she will perceive that remark as one of the five types of responses listed above. This may not correspond with what you intended, but it is their perception that is crucial as it is upon this basis that they act. Let us first, however, define the responses more carefully.

1. Aggressive Response

An aggressive response is seen by the receiver as an attack upon his personality, his beliefs, his facts, or anything that he identifies with, and which he feels is being undermined by the other person or persons in the conversation. In the above case, Ray Stevens began to feel under attack when Jim Walsh said 'that scrap-rate in your department needs looking at'. The words used by Walsh were seen by Stevens as a criticism of the way in which he had been managing the department.

2. Defensive Response

A defensive response is one that seeks to excuse, explain, justify, or rationalize a situation. It is in the nature of the defensive response, as the name implies, to stop the aggressive remarks of the other person going any further. In the above case, Stevens replied 'Don't forget that my department has all the old machines' when he felt under attack from Walsh.

3. Regressive Response

A regressive response is characterized by a person making a verbal or non-verbal withdrawal from the situation. This form of response is based on an individual's judgement that he has nothing further to contribute; is unable to cope; is bored; has other priorities to attend to; or wishes to avoid further interaction with the person or subject. At the end of the brief conversation in the case incident, Walsh began to withdraw on the issue of employing more people when he said, 'We can't take on any more labour just yet'. This statement indicated that as far as he was concerned this subject was not open to further immediate discussion as he wished to withdraw from the topic.

4. Fixative Response

A fixative response occurs when a person makes a remark that indicates that he is repeating the same point he has made before, regardless of its appropriateness or relevance to the current level of discussion. In effect, a person making a fixative response starts to go round in circles. He is occupied, to the exclusion of all else, by one point or issue which he reiterates.

5. Supportive Response

A supportive response is one which is perceived by the receiver as helping him to develop his ideas. It gives encouragement and helps to extend his problem-solving process. It is in this sense that a critical comment is seen as supportive, if the person receiving it perceives the comment to be given in a helpful spirit. As suggested in the discussion of Walsh and Stevens, Walsh could have been seen to be supportive by reflecting back Stevens's concern by saying 'You feel that having more men would help with the scrap-rate problem?'

The above examples refer, in the main, to verbal responses. The same principles also apply to behavioural responses, such as physical aggression and defence; physical withdrawal, as when a person removes himself from a room; physical fixation, as when a person keeps looking in the same place for his car keys; or physical support, as when a person helps another, say, by typing, mending a television, driving, or any other physical action. Although, in this context, we are concentrating on the verbal aspects, this does not mean that physical elements are unimportant. Indeed, there should in theory be a high correlation between words and deeds, although we all know in practice this does not always occur.

PROBLEM-SOLVING APPROACHES AND BEHAVIOURAL RESPONSES

So far, we have developed the view that whenever a person engages in conversation regarding a problem, his conversation is either problem-centred or solution-centred. In this chapter, we have introduced a further dimension, suggesting a number of behavioural responses that can occur in problem solving. It is the interaction between these two major factors that determines to a large degree the effectiveness of the problem-solving process.

Let us take an example to illustrate some of the possibilities. Imagine a conversation between a foreman Ray Shields and an operative Jim Wilson regarding overtime as shown in Fig. 7.1.

This case is not untypical of many discussions that take place in industry every day. However, in most of these discussions too much energy is wasted by both parties in trying to impose their solution on the other, rather than thinking how best to meet each other's needs.

It is only possible to make real progress when both parties to a problem perceive that it is in their interest to engage in a given behaviour. To impose tasks on others, where they have no say, is to ask for poor-quality work to be turned out. In Fig. 7.1, however, Shields started the conversation in a solution-orientated fashion by providing an incentive to Wilson for working overtime. This strategy of negotiation failed as Wilson had another objective

Discussion content	Shields's perception	Wilson's perception
SHIELDS: Jim, I would like you to work overtime tonight as one of the machines has broken down. It will give you a chance to earn some extra money.	NEGOTIATE/HELPING RESPONSE, i.e., to increase Wilson's pay	ATTACK on own plans
WILSON: I'd rather not work tonight.	WITHDRAWING	WITHDRAWING
SHIELDS: But I'm depending on you. We need that machine urgently. You are always asking for overtime. Here is your chance.	PRESCRIPTIVE ATTACK	ATTACK increased
WILSON: Not tonight, though, thanks. You haven't given me enough warning.	Still WITHDRAWING	Need to DEFEND
SHIELDS: How much warning do you want? It's only ten o'clock in the morning.	Move to ATTACK through CONSULTATIVE question	CONSULTATIVE ATTACK
WILSON: Maybe, but I'm going to a football match tonight and I'm not working for you or anyone else.	DIRECTIVE	DIRECTIVE
SHIELDS: That's no reason for not working. You know the company rules require you to work in an emergency like this?	ATTACK ATTACK using CONSULTATIVE question to inform Wilson of rules	ATTACK ATTACK
WILSON: As far as I'm concerned, my time is my own after five-thirty. You haven't given me twenty-four hours' notice according to the rules.	WITHDRAWAL Statement	WITHDRAWAL Statement
SHIELDS: Instead of us both getting angry, let's see if there is a way round the problem. How long will it take you to mend the oil filter on number 3 machine?	CONSULTATIVE/SUPPORTIVE	CONSULTATIVE/SUPPORTIVE
WILSON: About three hours if there are no complications.	CONSULTATIVE/SUPPORTIVE	CONSULTATIVE/SUPPORTIVE
SHIELDS: Well, if you started at five and left at seven o'clock, you could get to the match and then come back and finish it later.	PRESCRIPTIVE/SUPPORTIVE	PRESCRIPTIVE/SUPPORTIVE
WILSON: That's a good idea. Yes I'll do that and come in an hour earlier tomorrow and finish it.	DIRECTIVE/SUPPORTIVE	DIRECTIVE/SUPPORTIVE

which he felt took precedence over the offer from Shields. At this stage, Shields, having been rejected, found himself resorting to a strategy of threat to back up his negotiated offer. When this did not work because the rules were on Wilson's side, Shields posed the difficulty as a situational problem that both men could diagnose.

When Shields asked the question 'How long will it take you to mend the machine?', both men were able to consider the problem rather than bicker over Wilson's refusal. At this point, Shields, having assessed Wilson's objectives and the time constraint, felt able to prescribe a solution which Wilson accepted and took it upon himself to outline when the task should be completed.

The function of the case is to illustrate the dynamics of people's behaviour in a problem-solving situation. The critical skills required involve an understanding and ability to develop expertise in interpersonal problem solving. The response that you give to a person with whom you are seeking to resolve a problem will determine substantially his behaviour towards you. Whenever you find yourself in an interpersonal problem-solving position, it is important to ask what will be the effect if you respond in a particular way. Obviously, it is difficult to predict, but it is possible to outline some basic principles which should aid your choice of response.

This case, then, highlights the importance of recognizing how the other person perceives your communication. If he sees it as an attack upon his plans, as Wilson regarded Shields's remarks, he is likely to defend or withdraw. When Wilson did withdraw, Shields should have asked himself if this was the behaviour he wanted Wilson to engage in. If not, he should have questioned the validity of continuing to pursue the same line of discussion. If the other person concerned in a discussion starts to oppose or withdraw, then this response should be a sign that the nature of the communication, if not the content, must change.

Shields recognized that his communication was being seen as an attack, and perceived Wilson's need to withdraw. His change of tactics was to move to a problem-centred position where he asked supportive questions, indicating concern for Wilson's plans. At this point, the tenor of the conversation changed and a mutually satisfactory problem-solving discussion began.

Summary

A. In this chapter, attention has been drawn to the five major forms of response that can be seen to have importance in interpersonal problem solving. In this context, the chapter has indicated:
  • The difference between words and meaning.
  • The importance of language in problem solving.
  • The types of response to verbal communication.
  • The relation of these responses to problem-solving approaches.

B. In particular, the chapter should help the manager to:
   - Develop a recognition of the need to change tactics in meetings that result in one side attacking and the other withdrawing.
   - Assess the behavioural objectives and results of interpersonal problem-solving meetings.
C. In considering the issues raised, a manager should ask himself:
   - What sort of response do I wish to receive from the other person?
   - To what extent do my present tactics produce aggressive, defensive, regressive, fixative, or supportive behaviour from others?
   - Do I act upon these behaviour observations early or late in discussions?
   - How far do I feel able to express my personal feelings on the extent to which I react to the other person in aggressive, defensive, regressive, fixative, or supportive terms?

8

EXPRESSION AND DEVELOPMENT IN PROBLEM SOLVING

'I'm not sure I should tell you this,' said Jim Bird, a machine operator at the TAS Company, 'but I fixed the machine on number four line last week so we could get in some overtime.' Bird was talking to his section manager Len Alston in a meeting with all the other operatives present.

Alston was surprised by the comment and was unsure what to say. He had called the meeting because he was concerned about the high cost of production in his section during the six months he had been the manager. His objectives had been to increase productivity and reduce costs. So far, he had not achieved anything. He had therefore called a meeting and told the operatives his problem and his objectives. 'I would like us to have an honest discussion of the issues. I want to hear your views on what problems exist and ideas on how they can be solved.'

The meeting had been going on for an hour when Jim Bird, the most senior of the operatives, made his comment. The discussion had centred on the point made by Alston that one reason a problem existed was that his section worked a lot of overtime, but did not produce as much as others. 'We seem to get a lot of stoppages for breakdowns on our machines,' he said. Bird's comment was important in so far as the company regulations clearly stated that anyone involved in interfering with machinery to prevent it functioning would be automatically dismissed. As Alston listened to Bird he, and everyone else in the room, knew what the company policy was on such a matter.

ALTERNATIVE BEHAVIOURAL RESPONSE

According to the theory developed here, some of the options open to Alston were as follows:

1. 'You know, as does everyone else, that such fixing of machines is an infringement of company policy. I have no option but to dismiss you. You will get one week's wages in lieu of notice.'

2. 'You know the company rules on the matter. It's a serious offence. Regulations about interfering with machinery are made for your benefit. You should keep to those regulations.'

3. 'Look, we have got to have an understanding on the fixing of machines. I'm prepared to forget it this time, on the understanding that it doesn't happen again and you don't work unnecessary overtime.'

4. 'Yes, you are right, I'm not sure you should tell me that. It's a very serious thing to admit you fixed the machines. I'm not sure what I should do in the matter. Tell me what you thought you could achieve by doing it?'

5. 'You felt that you had to fix the machines to get in some overtime?'

The choice Alston makes at this point in the meeting is critical to the future relations he has with his operatives. In their discussion, Bird, the senior operative, felt confident enough to admit that he personally had contravened company regulations in order to achieve the operatives', as yet unstated, objectives. By making such a statement, he is taking a risk. Will Alston seize upon it to make a scapegoat of him, or will he take other routes? According to the theory outlined here, the major alternatives are as shown in Fig. 8.1.

Figures 1 to 5 on the matrix represent the type of response highlighted in the examples given above. For the purpose of analysis, a judgement on the interpretation of the manager's response has been made. Furthermore, it is assumed that Alston's intention in making the response would be interpreted in the same way by the recipients. Of course, in real life, this does not always occur. One can set out intending to be prescriptive in approach and supportive by, for example, suggesting to someone how he can improve his work. However, this may be interpreted by the recipient as directive behaviour and aggressive in which he, the recipient, is being criticized and commanded to do things differently in future. In the present examples, it is assumed that both the manager and the operatives perceive the communications in a similar manner.

The other point to stress is the wide range of possible response that a manager has. In the present model, there are twenty-five alternatives. The five selected therefore represent aspects of a complex picture. In addition, the words and phrases used would differ from person to person, even though they might choose the same area of response. However, the meaning of the message would be essentially the same. It is with these points in mind that we seek to examine the issues raised, should Alston decide to choose any of the present alternatives.

Perceived Responses

	Aggressive	Defensive	Regressive	Fixative	Supportive
DIRECTIVE	1				
PRESCRIPTIVE		2			
NEGOTIATIVE			3		
CONSULTATIVE				4	
REFLECTIVE					5

Problem-solving approach

Fig. 8.1   Alternative modes of interpersonal response

1. Directive/Aggressive Response

If Alston uses a directive and aggressive response, he is closing the door to immediate future discussions on his original objectives of increasing productivity and reducing costs. To 'throw the rulebook' at Bird is to punish the man who was brave and honest enough to raise one aspect of the reason why productivity was low and costs high. It is unlikely that other operatives will be willing to speak openly in any future meetings. Should Alston dismiss Bird, the operatives will hardly cooperate with a man who asks to hear their views, but dismisses those who tell the truth on issues of malpractice. Alston, however, would, of course, be within his legal rights to exert a directive/aggressive response in such a situation. Indeed, some would say he would not be doing his duty if he did not dismiss the man, regardless of future relationships with the operatives. However, by taking the solution-centred approach, what problem is Alston likely to solve? Will he stop the malpractice? Will productivity increase? Will costs decline?

2. Prescriptive/Defensive Response

If Alston adopted a prescriptive and defensive response to Bird's statement, he would essentially be defending company regulations and emphasizing that operatives should keep to the rules. While offering a strong suggestion to the operatives about their future conduct, he would be concerned to make the point that the rules were established in the men's interest. The central question, however, concerns the appropriateness of such a response. Bird has made an admission. He already knows the regulations. Reading a homily on the reason for the existence of the rules, and giving advice on how Bird should behave in the future, hardly deals with the substance of his comment. Indeed, those listening may question whether it is worth identifying themselves with the problems if the response they receive is simply the passing of a judgement upon their behaviour to the effect that they must not be such 'bad boys' in the future.

Alston has to consider what would be achieved by using the response. Would it help him to get more information on why the operatives felt it essential to work overtime? Would it help him reach the objectives he established at the beginning of the meeting? Is the discussion likely to be more free-flowing or more constrained if he uses the prescriptive-defensive approach?

3. Negotiative/Regressive Response

In the negotiative and regressive approach, Alston has the option of making a bargain with the operatives, that he will be prepared to forget the incident if the men do not do it again and stop working unnecessary overtime. Thus, while making a bargain, he is also saying 'let's withdraw from this topic'—in effect, let us regress.

Should Alston adopt this approach, it is important to consider what would happen to the conversation at the meeting. Bird, in announcing he has contravened the rules, has staked out the ground for discussion. This involves a risk both for the operatives and the manager. If Alston uses the negotiative/regressive approach, he is in essence saying he does not wish to pursue this topic, thereby indicating that the issue is 'too hot to handle'. If he does this, the operatives will know that the risk and trust boundaries of the discussion have been reached. While Bird's comment may have been true, and central to the issue of high costs and low productivity, Alston's adoption of this approach would rule it out of court for further discussion.

Clearly, Alston has to question what results would be achieved by using this approach. Would the negotiative/regressive approach facilitate a clearer diagnosis of the problem? Would it encourage the operatives to be more open in their relationship with the manager? Would such an approach aid Alston in reaching his objectives as stated at the beginning of the meeting?

4. Consultative/Fixative Response

The consultative and fixative response would indicate that the manager is not exactly sure what to do or which way to proceed. He is fixating; perhaps stalling for time. Alston would repeat the doubt expressed by Bird, who said he wasn't sure whether to divulge the malpractice. The manager would then say he was not sure what to do and eventually end up by asking the operative what he thought he could achieve by the malpractice.

By taking this approach, Alston may feel he can best express his honest doubts. If he doesn't know what to do or cannot understand Bird's motivation, he may feel that to say so is the best way of coping with a situation which has caught him unprepared.

However, Alston would need to consider the possible effect of such a response on the operatives. Bird already had doubts, knowing as he did the penalties for malpractice, of expressing his point. If Alston seems to support Bird's reservations on such expression, then he may well reinforce the operative's original concern about the effect of publishing such potentially explosive information. Moreover, what effect will a consultative/fixative approach have on the other operatives? Will they see the manager as someone not able or prepared to discuss the reasons for malpractice? If this should happen, it is unlikely that they will volunteer information which may endanger themselves. Bird's comment will undoubtedly be taken as a test case on how far they should go. If the manager handles the issue with discretion and trust, it is possible that others may venture forth with more of the truth regarding the low productivity and high costs. However, should the manager be hesitant, unsure of how to cope, or imply a critical judgement in his questions, the operatives will be doubtful as to how far they can trust him. They will question whose side he is on, and where there is any suspicion that he is not *for* them it is unlikely that future meetings will be successful.

Alston would, therefore, have to consider the extent to which the consultative/fixative approach would aid or hinder the discussion.

5. Reflective/Supportive Response

If Alston uses the reflective and supportive response, he is letting Bird know he has heard his comment and would like him to continue. This approach, in effect, gives the conversation back to Bird. The nature of Alston's option therefore is to isolate the concern expressed by Bird and indicate to him his awareness of it and interest in hearing more.

This option does not involve making any judgement about Bird's statement. It does, however, involve a willingness to listen, without intervention to praise, criticize, or show surprise. It involves a concern to let the other person say what he wishes to say. The reflective/supportive approach therefore, in this instance, should indicate to the other person that it is permissible to speak one's mind, without fear of reprisal.

In some ways, this approach could be seen as a negative rather than supportive one. After all, the manager does not add anything to the operative's last statement. But what should the manager add? Who should be speaking? If the operatives have information on why productivity is low and costs high, then surely it is they who should control the conversation. In such circumstances, the manager's task is to be problem-centred and to listen rather than talk.

If this is so, then the question is how can this be achieved? What effect will the reflective/supportive response have? If the operatives receive the message that the manager is genuinely interested in what they have to say, and is prepared to deal with the problem rather than attack individuals, then it is likely that they will be prepared to help in the problem solving. Clearly, this is but a start, not a conclusion. Problems such as the one Alston put to his group are not solved easily, but it is vital to produce a climate of free expression to allow the problem-solving discussion to take place. It is incumbent upon the manager to take a lead in establishing such a climate. In this case, Alston would have to question how far this could be achieved by saying to Bird, 'You felt that you had to fix the machine to get in some overtime? Will this lead Bird to come forward with more information? Will such a response lower the suspicion level and heighten the trust between Alston and his group? Is it likely that such a response will enable the original problem of productivity and costs to be tackled?'

DEVELOPING A PROBLEM-SOLVING CLIMATE

So far, we have examined some alternative responses that a manager can make in dealing with a difficult problem. The central element in this discussion concerns how a manager can create a problem-solving climate where people are willing to share information freely and where mutual trust is high. There are no easy foolproof methods and certainly no one best way. There are, as indicated, a number of different approaches that can be used, and each person will make his judgement of what is the most likely to succeed on a given problem. That having been said, it is possible to indicate some guidelines on the alternative approaches that are likely to be more appropriate at certain stages of the problem-solving process.

In the case described, for example, Bird's remark that he had deliberately fixed the machine to enable overtime to be worked was of more than passing significance. It was not the sort of statement to be made lightly. In this sense, it was an important *cue* in the discussion. During any such discussion on business problems, invariably one, two, or maybe more, critical comments are made. The manner in which these comments are dealt with can be vital to the success or failure of the problem-solving process. Let us examine some aspects of this, by looking at some other cases.

Discretion

Andy Long, a marketing manager, had a lot of work to do. He therefore called his deputy Bill Fraser into his office. 'Bill, I want you to take these marketing reports and let me have an analysis of what the consumers think about the trial products we asked them to assess. I need the findings by next Friday. Let me know if you have any problems. If you want to see how I've done it in the past, have a look at the files.'

Bill Fraser picked up the reports. He had enough work on without this extra job. However, he had not had the experience of doing such a task before and felt it would be useful to learn it. He had a look at the previous work, but felt he could make an improvement on analysing the data. He, therefore, worked out a new coding system and set to work.

Two days later his boss, Andy Long, walked in to his office. 'How's that job going that I gave you?' he asked. 'Fine,' replied Fraser, 'the only problem is that it's taking up a lot of time. Maybe you could give me some extra help to get it completed by Friday. I think that I've begun to find some useful information which could really help our sales.'

Long looked at Fraser's desk. 'No wonder it's taking a long time. You are not using the system I told you to get from the files. Why can't you just do it the way I said? Look, I need the stuff urgently; you had better give it back to me.'

Here is a case where a manager has given his subordinate a job, but when the latter exercises his discretion he is criticized and has the job taken away. What effect is such behaviour likely to have on Fraser's future attempts at problem solving? Admittedly, he had tried his own approach without consultation, but what should Long have done in the circumstances?

In this case, Long took a directive/aggressive approach, adopting a solution-centred rather than a problem-centred behaviour. He ignored altogether Fraser's remark about finding 'useful information' which could help further sales. Fraser had introduced an 'important cue' which Long either had not heard or ignored. Long could have used this comment to adopt a problem-centred approach to discover what Fraser meant. In this way, he would have begun to understand how Fraser had used his discretion.

In effect, Long's action curtailed Fraser's freedom of expression. Long insisted on the necessity to keep to routine (accepted or traditional solutions) rather than experiment with alternative problem-solving approaches. His decision may have been correct, given the time pressures. However, his reaction may have been due to his low tolerance for ambiguity.

Tolerance of Ambiguity

By giving Fraser the task, Long had decreased his immediate control over the project. When he checked on Fraser's efforts two days later, he found that he did not understand what Fraser was doing. He was not using the accepted routine and things seemed to be getting out of control in terms of the time schedule. Long's reaction was to try and take control of the situation personally. This indicates that Long was not able to cope with an ambiguous situation. He felt unable to explore the new method with Fraser. He therefore sought to reduce the ambiguity by doing the task himself.

Tolerance for ambiguous situations, however, is important in problem-solving situations. Whenever one takes a new route or tries a new method, there is a degree of uncertainty. It is those people who can come to terms with the uncertainty through a considered analysis of the situation who are likely to solve the problem. However, in such situations there is usually a tendency to reduce risks by adopting the well tried and familiar. It is like being in a foreign country. One is usually happier when it is possible to resort to one's native tongue, rather than fumble for words in another language.

Important Cues

Both of the above cases point to the necessity to listen for and build upon important cues. In the first case, Bird referred to the fact that he 'fixed the machine'. In the second case, Fraser referred to 'useful information which could really help our sales'. For a manager concerned with furthering the problem-solving process, both these phrases are important cues.

Upon hearing such words, you, as manager, should recognize the importance of becoming problem-centred in approach. This will mean:

- Asking questions without implying judgement.
- Reflecting back the other person's concerns and feelings.
- Allowing the other person the freedom to develop his views, even though you may disagree with them, without interruption and before putting forward your own views.
- Helping the other person to clarify his thinking.
- Encouraging the other person to take risks.
- Extending a confidential relationship wherein mutual trust can develop.

Parallel and Sequential Conversations

Important cues can be recognized in a number of ways. Individuals are usually making a particularly significant contribution to the discussion when they start talking about themselves, using words such as 'I' or 'my' interests, values, objectives, or behaviour. Here, they are prepared to take the risk of talking about the one person who they really know well, and are concerned about—themselves. To be able to pick up such basic verbal cues and turn them into problem-centred discussion is a valuable skill.

Too often the opportunity is missed. Bird, for example, might say that he 'fixed the machine', and the manager could as we have seen close down the conversation by a variety of means. Another example that many of us are familiar with is the scene that is played out when the husband returns home from a hard and frustrating day's work in which he has expended a lot of effort, but feels he has achieved little. Upon entering the house, he is encountered by his wife who says 'Thank goodness you're home. I was hoping you would be early tonight. I've had a terrible day; the washing machine's broken down and I don't feel well.'

Clearly, this is a situation of high stress. The wife has given a number of verbal cues that she has problems that require further discussion in a problem-centred manner. If, however, the husband says in reply, 'You think you have had a bad day, I've had nothing but trouble since I left home. You are not the only one who has had a bad day'.

Has this really helped? Is it likely to aid the problem-solving process? In effect, we have here an example of a *parallel* conversation. Neither person is prepared to listen or talk about the other's problem. The discussion runs on *parallel* lines as shown below:

Person A
My problem is important because . . . .
Person B
My problem is just as important . . . .
Person A
Well . . . .

The alternative is for person B in such a situation to be sensitive to the initial cue and pick up the comment in a problem-centred way to facilitate the problem-solving process. This would then become a *sequential* conversation which would develop as follows:

Person A	Person B
My problem is important because	*Tell me more* . . . .

If person A and person B compete to get the other to listen and to help them express their feelings, then it is unlikely that either will get far in the problem-solving process.

Implicit in what is being said here is that when the problem solving involves highly emotional issues, questions of personal values, or just obscurity as to the means and ends of the process, then talking the problem through can be most helpful. The discussion process with someone who can focus on problem-centred questions and comments can often clear one's thinking, even if the other person makes no attempt at offering a solution.

Conclusion

In this chapter, there has been a heavy emphasis on the need to examine responses in relation to the consequence or result that it is wished to attain from the other person. The focus in the cases we have examined has been primarily on developing a problem-centred focus, given the alternatives available.

Summary

A. In this chapter, attention has been drawn to freedom of expression, whereby consideration of the following issues has taken place:
- The relationship of problem-solving approaches and interpersonal style.
- Factors important in developing a problem-solving climate.
- The relationship of language to freedom of expression.
- Aspects of problem-solving skills.

B. In particular, the chapter should enable the manager to:
- Assess the alternative approaches and possible responses likely in a problem-solving discussion.
- Identify the conditions for freedom of expression and personal development.
- Recognize parallel and sequential conversation.
- Assess the implications of problem-centred and solution-centred responses.

C. In considering the issues raised, a manager should ask himself:
- What sort of responses do I receive in problem-solving discussions?
- What situations do I create to allow others freedom of expression and development?
- What level of discretion do I allow?
- How do I cope with ambiguity?
- Do I recognize verbal and behavioural cues?

9

MANAGERIAL INFLUENCE

SUPPORT AND ENCOURAGEMENT

How important is it for a manager to support and encourage his colleagues and subordinates? Research increasingly indicates that these factors may be of considerable significance in the way others perform. The theory is called the 'self-fulfilling prophecy'.

This theory states quite simply that people will behave as you expect them to behave. Therefore, if you prophesy that the job will go well and that it will be a success, then there is a high likelihood of that prophecy coming true. If, on the other hand, you express doubt and say that you feel uncertain, then this attitude affects others and they will behave in accordance with your expectations.

Now, this theory has been tested and found in a number of situations to have some basis in reality. Alex Bavelas has shown that in a large industrial company the expectations foremen had of their subordinates significantly affected output. The foremen were told that certain operatives had scored higher on a special test designed to show aptitude for their job. In fact, these people had been chosen at random. However, two things occurred. When the foremen were later asked to evaluate their subordinates, they chose the randomly selected people, whom they had been told had done well on the test, as their best workers. Furthermore, when the production records were examined, it was found that this group had a superior production output record. Subsequent experiments have supported these findings, which suggests that if a person of influence expects others to perform well and conveys this expectation to them, then it will become a self-fulfilling prophecy.

This theory has possible application in the group problem-solving process. Let us therefore consider in more depth the range of decision response identified in chapter 8 which managers should consider in discussions in which they are concerned to help others improve job performance.

Decision Tone

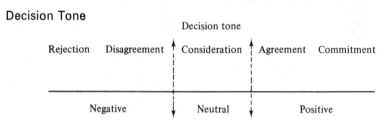

Fig. 9.1   Attitudes to others' performance

We shall define the terms on the scale in Fig. 9.1 in the following way:

1. *Rejection*   Here, a manager is defiant, rejecting the work of his subordinates and colleagues. When ideas are put to him by his co-workers he dismisses them. When he is requested to help he always has a prior commitment or excuse. He is seen by his colleagues and subordinates to be out to defeat their ideas. This is likely to lead to the development of a win/lose conflict.

2. *Disagreement*   The manager adopting this approach indicates that he feels doubtful about the success of a given idea or project. He will take an interest in the discussions, but will look critically at the proposals. He will normally express his concern by asking questions which imply an answer that negates the idea or project. His questioning, critical, sceptical outlook may be beneficial to the problem-solving process in that it highlights areas for further research and effort. However, his attitude is unlikely to develop *esprit de corps* or high motivation among his colleagues and subordinates. Indeed, the sceptic's approach, expressing doubt, may lead to the self-fulfilling prophecy occurring as others lose their motivation.

3. *Consideration*   This approach is a middle-ground position. The manager does not encourage or discourage his colleagues or subordinates. He does not make or imply judgements of the worth of the others' ideas or projects. He tries to adopt a neutral position, sometimes seen as fence-sitting. This will involve behaviour such as asking for information, listening to the expression of views, and making factual comments on specific issues when asked questions. He will let the other person lead the conversation. On no occasions does he adopt a solution-centred approach. When asked his opinion, he will respond that he does not have sufficient knowledge to make a comment. The 'fence-sitter' is not detached, he will express a 'scientific'

interest in ideas and projects by seeking knowledge on their development and prospects. This, however, does not indicate his support or dismissal of the ideas or projects.

4. *Agreement* The manager adopting this approach will exhibit a belief that the ideas or projects being put forward have in his opinion a probability of success. He will express support for propositions, and will talk and act as if he expected the venture to succeed. He will encourage others in words and deeds. Although he is confident, he is aware of the possibility of failure. Even so, he is prepared to risk his time, energy, and other resources that he feels he can afford, such as money and machines, in support of a venture.

5. *Commitment* The manager taking this position has a firm trust, belief, and faith that the ideas or projects are right. He has a conviction that the path being trod is the proper one. He sees the probability of failure as negligible, the probability of success as all but certain. He commits himself and his resources to the ideas or projects with little reservation, provided he accepts their importance. He encourages others to have the same faith in them as he does. His faith will be regarded by some as not being based on reality, and he will therefore be regarded in some quarters as a bigot. Indeed, the person with such convictions may only look for information that supports his belief, and consider as unrepresentative those facts that do not accord with his position. The really convinced person can develop his own reality and live in a 'world of his own'. This, however, is extreme. It is normal for a person to be convinced, yet retain a critical judgement on events as they occur and reassess his position if the information warrants it. However, where there is an ambiguity, the convinced person will not hesitate to give his support to the ideas or projects.

COMMUNICATION AND REACTION

In order to examine the model of managerial influence, let us take a case incident. This will involve John Franklin who was asked to make a report on the high number of sub-standard products being produced in one section of the factory. Franklin wrote a report which he submitted to his colleagues at the next works management meeting. He concluded as follows:

'The results of the work study show that the operatives are not adopting the most efficient approach to their job. The present procedures, it is believed, contribute substantially to the high number of rejects due to the excessive number of movements required to do the work. It has, therefore, been suggested in the main body of the report that the job be reorganized and all the operatives be given a special two-day course in the new methods.'

After Franklin had spoken on his report he listened carefully to the responses of his colleagues. They each, he felt, took different positions. During the discussion, the following comments were made:

PRODUCTION MANAGER: I believe this report points to the real issues involved. I am in favour of introducing these new methods and feel that productivity will go up to more than meet the lost output and cost of training. This, I feel, is an urgent matter which we must decide upon today.

TRAINING MANAGER: It seems to me a very clear and well-produced report. I am willing to help on the training side in any way. I feel that with good training we could make a major investment here to improve the efficiency and productivity of the plant.

WORKS MANAGER: I don't think we should waste time on this as within the next six months we are planning to introduce new machines into the production area under discussion. This is recent information as a result of my visit to the trade fair. This report may be out-of-date. Perhaps we need more information on the skills required for manning the new machines?

WORKS ACCOUNTANT: Mr Franklin's proposals are deficient in so far as they ignore the financial side. I'm not sure that we should rush into this proposal. The cost of the training and the loss of production revenue will be substantial. However, a possible hidden cost is the wage claims that will possibly come once the jobs have been reassessed. Also, given the point just made by the works manager, I feel doubtful about the financial value of Mr Franklin's proposal, particularly when we are likely to have a major outlay shortly.

WORKS ENGINEER: I don't know what this report means by job changes, and even less about what effect training will have on performance. I'm busy evaluating these new machines that have been mentioned. It will take me a month and I will let you have a report on them.

Each of these responses reflects one aspect of the attitudes referred to in the model shown in Fig. 9.1. The production manager is *convinced* of the appropriateness of Franklin's proposals. The training manager is *confident* that he can produce an effective training programme that will cope with the problem. The works manager rejects the report. He does not wish to decide either way on Franklin's proposals until decisions have been made on the new machine. The works accountant, however, is *sceptical* of both the value and timing of Franklin's proposal, given the information on new machines. The works engineer is not really interested in Franklin's proposals. His concern is with his own technical review of the new machines.

The responses given above by the works manager and his colleagues are illustrative of possible comments to reflect the ways in which managers seek to influence other people's ideas or projects. They serve to indicate the range of alternative responses managers can make. This analysis is intended to highlight the importance of the effect of such responses on subordinates and others. Scepticism may be the way to convince a person that his ideas are not good enough or even impractical, while fence-sitting may knock the steam and energy out of his enthusiasm. In short, to cast doubt on ideas may be a self fulfilling prophecy ensuring that they are not developed to the full. Indeed, it is possible that a person may come to you with his ideas only to gain the confidence to continue exploring and experimenting.

On occasions, however, it is possible that a good deal of scepticism itself can act as a motivator. If a person feels his ideas or projects are under attack, he may well go back and try all the harder to prove their worth. This type of person is resilient and capable of sustaining his effort in the face of others' doubt and criticism. Many people are not like this. They need encouragement and support if their ideas are to take off.

How, then, should one behave when there are real doubts about the worth of an idea? What should be done when factual evidence exists to contradict the assertions being made for a given project? How does one sustain motivation when a person is not performing as well as you could wish?

Taking Sides

It is valuable here to reconsider the concepts of problem-centred and solution-centred behaviour. If you have doubts about the viability of a project, perhaps the initial step is to express your concern in a problem-centred fashion without making value judgements as to the worth of the idea itself.

Let us look back at the comments made, for example, by the works manager on Franklin's report. He adopts a problem-centred attitude, but makes some unnecessary (deflating) value judgements. He says 'I don't think we should *waste time* on this'. Later, he remarks 'This report may be out of date'. Neither of these comments is destined to inspire Franklin with the motivation to do another report. Instead, the works manager could have given his information about new machines without additional judgement and comments.

Likewise, the works accountant could have pointed to the financial costs involved without making an explicit judgement attack on the quality of the report. He could have offered his information and suggested that it be included in a redrafted version.

There is a difference of emphasis in disagreeing with someone and being sceptical in a judgemental fashion. Likewise, there is a difference between accepting another person's viewpoint and expressing a judgement of confidence in the direction he is proceeding. It is the attitude a manager takes to others, and the way in which he deals with them, that *influences* their behaviour. There is in this an emotional element which goes beyond the intellectual rights and wrongs. In agreeing or disagreeing, one is putting oneself into a relationship with another person, in which he asks 'whose side is he on?'.

For the manager, it is critical that he is seen to be on the side of his colleagues and subordinates. Without their support and cooperation he will cease to manage. Yet, if he is seen to be genuinely intending to assist, it is likely that his words and actions will have a bearing on the behaviour of others.

Prophecy or Criticism

The point here is that people with managerial influence have the ability to make prophecies come true. They are the force behind the self-fulfilling prophecy. Every football manager knows this. It is his central task to make his team *believe* they can win. His task is to give them the confidence and conviction to match their technical ability.

The successful manager will, for each criticism, have words of encouragement for his players; words of praise; statements of intent; affirmations of faith; assurances of belief; and above all prophecies of success. This is not to say successful managers do not criticize. They do. But research in industry indicates that criticism by itself has no significant effect towards improving performance.

Criticism, by and large, says what not to do. It emphasizes the negative. Prophecy of success, words of praise, and affirmations of faith and belief emphasize positive things. If the theory of the self-fulfilling prophecy is correct, it may be that more emphasis ought to be put on accentuating the strong points in people's behaviour than the weak points.

All this is easier said than done, and for many people it is controversial as an approach to management. The test is in practice, not in theory. Only people like yourself who read this can discover whether the theory has any substance. The manager has the opportunity to put behavioural science to work and assess its value in one major area.

It takes courage and an ability to restrain critical faculties. But it could be worth a try. Use comments such as 'I like this pattern' or 'I think that idea you put forward yesterday is worth exploring further'. If it is important to point someone's attention to errors or areas of omission, then possibly the approach may be as follows: 'I like that pattern. I need more of that quality'. Then point out what you mean by 'that quality'. Alternatively, 'I think the idea you put forward yesterday is worth exploring further. Could you get the financial aspects worked out by tomorrow so we can take it further?'

Come-Ons and Knock-Downs

The way a manager uses language is important. Words can encourage a person to come forward, develop his ideas, and try harder, or they can deflate and knock down his efforts.

It is not even necessary to praise a person to encourage him to develop his ideas. An open-ended question can be the vital sign he is looking for to show you are interested.

Fred Hopkins was a junior manager in the training department of a large electronics company. The production manager, John Kirk, asked him to design a training programme for the inspectors in the department who he felt were not as quick as they should be at their work. Hopkins studied the inspectors' work and then went to see Kirk: 'I've assessed the work of your inspectors. In my view, more training would have little effect. What we require is a reorganization and redeployment of labour.'

At this point, Kirk's response is important. He could reply as follows: 'Look, I'm not interested in turning the department upside down. All I want is you to help the inspectors increase their speed by giving them a training programme.' Alternatively, he could say 'Tell me more about these ideas'.

The first response is something of a 'knock-down', a 'do-as-you're-told' type of comment. This is hardly likely to motivate Hopkins. The second comment, however, makes no immediate judgement other than to ask for information. The effect is to encourage Hopkins to come forward and develop his ideas. In the process, he is likely to gather confidence and extend his thinking on the practicality of his ideas.

The language used and interest shown, then, can be vital factors, determining the extent to which a manager is successful in influencing other people's behaviour. For some, saying the right things at the right time comes easily. It is a skill they have learnt over a long period, stretching back to their childhood. For others, the appropriate use of words is complex and difficult. Like all such skills, it can only be developed by practice and examining the responses other people make to you in day to day discussions.

'What will the "Old Man" say?'

The above phrase is well known in most organizations. A person has an idea. He may discuss this with other colleagues just to test it out. After they have explored the various issues, a decision is needed on what future action should be taken. Is there any use in putting the idea to the boss?

How many good ideas get lost because subordinates do not have sufficient confidence that the boss will give them a fair hearing?

The extent to which a manager gets to hear of good ideas could well be the result of how he treated those people who came to him with ideas previously. Did he knock them down and make them feel foolish? Or did he listen, support, and encourage?

It is a common complaint of many managers that their subordinates are not sufficiently creative, or do not come up with new and challenging ideas. Perhaps the ideas are there but the manager has not created the climate or situation within which they can flourish?

Clearly, it is not possible to say 'Yes' to every idea or suggestion. It is, however, possible to listen and to encourage people by showing an interest in their reasoning, even if in some cases action is not feasible. It is in the manner and in the tone that people tend to judge each other as much as by the decision that is made. In this sense, it is vital that managers understand the importance of the problem-solving process in terms of the self-fulfilling prophecy.

Summary

A. In this chapter, attention has been drawn to the importance of the self-fulfilling prophecy in management. Consideration of the following issues has taken place:
  - The importance of belief in achieving objectives.
  - The tone of interpersonal verbal expression.
  - The effect of judgements.
  - The issue of taking sides.
B. In particular, the chapter should enable the manager to:
  - Assess the importance of his behaviour in relation to colleagues and subordinates.
  - Be aware of the language that leads to a 'knock-down'.
  - Recognize the strength of the self-fulfilling prophecy.
C. In considering the issues raised, a manager should ask himself:
  - Is there an example in my work relations of the self-fulfilling prophecy?
  - How do my colleagues and subordinates perceive me—as a helpful person to talk to or as a 'knock-down' specialist?
  - What should I do to improve my social skills in these areas?

10

BEHAVIOURAL DECISION MAKING

INTERPERSONAL PROBLEM SOLVING AND DECISION MAKING

In any discussion, decisions have to be taken. When you say something, the other person has to decide what to say in response, and the tone in which to communicate. Chapter 9 identified some of the issues in the decision process in terms of managerial influence. This chapter takes the subject further and looks at how decisions develop in group problem-solving meetings.

Let us examine a problem confronted by Ralph Thorne. He was in charge of the warehouse and distribution facilities for the Domestic Products Co. One of his major problems was to make sure that sufficient products were distributed to each of the five sales areas each week. His job was to liaise with the production department and make sure sufficient stocks were kept.

One Monday afternoon, the manager of area A rang Ralph Thorne, and told him there was a problem. 'The stock you sent up this morning hasn't arrived. The driver got caught in fog on the motorway and was involved in a crash. He got out, but the lorry was burnt. This means we are in trouble. I want you to send me another consignment tonight, otherwise we are going to lose a lot of customers.'

Ralph Thorne had to make a behavioural decision. He could reply in one of the following ways, accepting or rejecting the request:

1. 'That suggestion of yours is impossible. I can't do it. I've only enough stock in to supply area B who have a delivery on Wednesday.'

2. 'I don't think your idea will solve the problem. We haven't got enough stock in. I think you should see what you can buy in from local manufacturers.'

3. 'It will be a bit difficult sending you another load tonight. I've only got enough stock for area B's delivery on Wednesday. Leave it with me, though, and I will see if we can't increase production and then I can give you some of the area B stock.'

4. 'OK, I see your problem. I will do what I can to get some stock to you tonight, but you may have to wait till tomorrow.'

5. 'Leave it to me. I will get the lads to load a new lorry. It means robbing area B's stock, but I'll take the risk that production can make up the loss by Wednesday. You should have the delivery by 6.00 PM.'

Let us look at this case more carefully.

Interpersonal Problem-Solving Distance

To examine the above case, we shall look at the model of interpersonal problem-solving distance. This is based on the response alternatives identified in chapter 9.

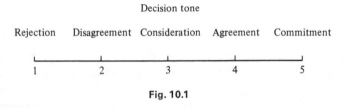

Fig. 10.1

In between these points, there are variations of response, in which there is neither total acceptance or rejection. In this formulation, it is assumed that the more you are prepared to accept the other person's response, the more you are likely to be committed. The critical issue in interpersonal problem solving is whether over a period of time (a problem-solving meeting, for instance) people move closer together in their views or farther apart.

The perceptions people have of each other's communication influence the decisions they make on such things as what to say next, whether to continue the conversation, and their active commitment to resolve a problem.

The decision response in any conversation can be assessed as indicated previously:

1. *Rejection* This is an outright refusal to go any further with either a request or a statement on the opinion, information, or action under discussion.

2. *Disagreement* This is a denial of any proposition put forward, but contains a willingness to continue the communication, presumably on common ground.

3. *Consideration*   This is a point at which a person is willing to think about a request or statement, but not accept or reject the other's opinion, knowledge, or action until more is known.

4. *Agreement*   This is an expression of concord, whereby one person accepts the validity of the other's opinion, knowledge, or action.

5. *Commitment*   This is where a decision is taken on the substance of the opinions, knowledge, and actions that reflects itself in a commitment to implementing the decision.

The concept of interpersonal problem-solving distance (IPS distance) assumes that people have different views, and/or objectives. The greater the difference, the greater will be the IPS distance between them. The responses that people make in problem-solving meetings will either reduce or accentuate this difference.

In the above example, Ralph Thorne, like any manager, has a number of possible alternative responses he can make. In response 1, he completely rejects the suggestion from the area A manager. Response 2 is not a total rejection. Thorne disagrees with the area manager's suggestion about sending another consignment, but offers him an alternative solution. In response 3, Thorne considers the solution of the area manager. He asks for time to look into the matter before deciding finally. He wishes to gather more information before choosing whether to move towards the rejection or the commitment end of the scale. The alternative in response 4 is to accept the solution put forward by the area manager. Thorne, nevertheless, seeks to give himself time by saying that the delivery may not be made till the following day. In response 5, Thorne commits himself to the area manager's proposal. This involves, as he says, taking a risk, but he is willing, without reservation, to try to get the consignment to area A by 6.00 PM.

Rejection and Commitment

Why do people reject or accept your views and ideas? People can be inclined to reject your views for a number of reasons. As indicated in previous chapters, this may be because they have other objectives, different time demands, or alternative diagnoses of the problem and solutions. Furthermore, others may not like your interpersonal relations approach. They may feel that you are being problem-centred when they want you to be solution-centred or vice-versa. They may perceive your communication as aggressive when you mean to be supportive. There are many interpersonal and other factors that lead to the taking up of positions on the rejection–commitment scale.

If the other person concerned is committed, then he may share your objectives, time horizons, and plans. On the other hand, he may feel he is getting a good bargain, or is not involved in much risk, by going along with the ideas. Other factors that can lead to the commitment of others to your ideas may be that they have trust and confidence in what you say, and the manner in which you say it. If you adopt the appropriate problem-centred and solution-centred responses for the person involved, and are perceived to be supportive, then it is likely you will receive more commitment to the views you express.

Let us, however, examine some discussions and identify some of the ways in which conversation can develop.

INTERPERSONAL PROBLEM-SOLVING DISCUSSIONS

In all conversations concerned with problems, people are either moving towards some common understanding, remaining very much in the same situation at which they started, or moving further away from each other. The aim here is to look at how conversation develops over time and identify various forms of problem-solving discussions.

1. Polarization Effect

Where two parties in a problem-solving meeting insist on the correctness of their own position, refuse to listen to each other's comments, criticize each other's statements, and seek to prove the superiority of their own position, then the interpersonal problem-solving distance is likely to increase, and the gap between the parties will be wider at the conclusion of the meeting than at the beginning. This is due to the fact that rejection by one party of the other's case tends to lead to the other party reciprocating in a similar way. This is shown diagrammatically in Fig. 10.2.

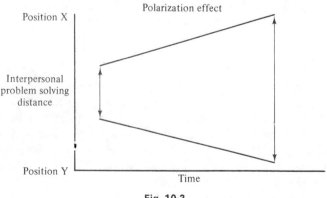

Fig. 10.2

An example of this sort of discussion is reflected in the following problem between two managers who are working on a joint venture:

MANAGER A: I think we should get this job finished by April at the latest.
MANAGER B: I agree it's important to get it finished, but that's rushing it too much.

MANAGER A: April seems fine to me. If we get organized and allocate time to the project, we will make it easy.

MANAGER B: I don't think we have enough knowledge to say that we will finish in April. I would rather leave the date open.

MANAGER A: That means we will keep putting it off. Unless we have a deadline we will not get it done.

MANAGER B: That may be all right for you, but I have a lot of other jobs to do.

MANAGER A: I'm in exactly the same situation, but I'm not complaining. Let's stop arguing and start working.

MANAGER B: I don't think you understand . . . .

MANAGER A: I understand time is short. What we need is action.

MANAGER B: Well, unless we can reassess the time schedule on this I will have to let you get on with it either by yourself or someone else.

Clearly, the conversation is not producing a mutual agreement or commitment to action. If anything, the parties are moving away from each other. Initially, B agreed that it was important to get finished. At the end, he was threatening to withdraw.

The polarization effect occurs in many conversations. People meet with solid intentions of reaching agreement, but finish even further apart than when they began. If this begins to occur in your discussion, it may be a useful tactic to say, 'I don't feel we are making much progress on this. Perhaps we ought to look at the reasons underlying our difference of views.' In short, it may be of more value to stop the discussion and try to get at the factors blocking progress, rather than pursue a divisive discussion.

2. Fixation Effect
Both parties here take up fixed positions and conduct a meeting which reinforces their original differences. Neither side is prepared to give way; neither side generates new information: neither side takes up new opinions;

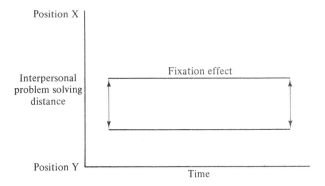

Fig. 10.3

and neither side proposes new initiatives or solutions. Instead, the meeting is a recapitulation of the arguments advanced from previous meetings. Both parties are fixated in that they repeat the behaviour exhibited before, even though they recognize it has been unsuccessful (Fig. 10.3).

This sort of meeting often characterizes the meetings between management and employee representatives. Each side is reluctant to give any ground, and for long periods the discussion can become fixated, as indicated in the case incident below:

EMPLOYEE REPRESENTATIVE: I have discussed with our members the offer that you made to us at our last meeting. They are not however prepared to accept less than the 10 per cent originally demanded.

MANAGEMENT REPRESENTATIVE: I'm disappointed. I thought our offer was fair. We certainly cannot go beyond our 5 per cent. As I told you last time, this would jeopardize the financial position of the company.

EMPLOYEE REPRESENTATIVE: Our situation has not changed either. As I told you before, it is vital that my members receive the 10 per cent claim not only to keep up with inflationary prices, but as a fair deal for the productivity improvements.

A conversation like this is going over 'old ground'. The previous positions are restated and held. Neither party is prepared to move. No new ideas are being generated. The discussion is in a state of fixation. The IPS distance between the parties remains constant. There is little problem solving. The conversation is running on parallel lines, with neither party being prepared to move to a point for mutual agreement.

3. Persuasion Effect

In this type of problem-solving meeting there is not only agreement, but both parties move in the direction of the position held by one of them. The characteristics of this form of meeting are that people are prepared to listen, to be flexible, to judge on evidence, not to be bound by prejudice, and to risk taking up new attitudes and behaviour. The persuasion effect may occur not because of a forceful argument of one party over the other, but because both parties, by sharing information and listening to each other, realize they have common goals and can agree on a particular way to resolve a problem. The term 'persuasion effect', therefore, may mean that one party may change its views towards those of the other, without the latter changing its position (Fig. 10.4).

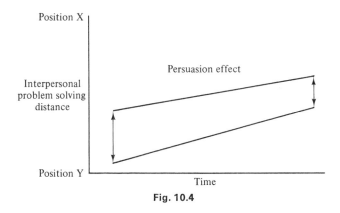

Fig. 10.4

The persuasion effect can occur for a number of reasons. One speaker may have more status and influence; be able to offer a reward for compliance; or produce more information and ideas which appeal to the other person. Whenever we are buying something, such as a car or a foreign holiday, we may change our mind if the other person can show us the value of purchasing the particular product he is recommending. In problem-solving meetings, such as that between manager A and manager B, the conversation may change somewhat like this:

MANAGER A: I think we could get the project finished by April, if we got some extra help with the routine administrative work. Look, I can afford to hire a temporary secretary to cope with the general stuff.

MANAGER B: OK, that sounds better. If we can organize it so that we don't spend hours coding all those cards, then I think we could aim for April. When can you get this person in to do the job?

The persuasion effect is difficult to achieve in many cases. It is dependent on an understanding of the other person's problems and the development of a creative solution that can resolve those problems and achieve the objective.

4. Compromise Effect

Here, both parties in the problem situation are prepared to listen to each other's case and, where appropriate, take steps to close the gap between them. If both parties do this, then a compromise effect occurs where each gives way in order to meet on the common ground where both can agree. The compromise effect is invariably the function of a negotiation where one party agrees to change if the counterpart in the discussion will do so. To this end, both move away from their original position, but achieve a basis for agreement and action on the problem. The compromise effect is most likely to occur when both parties have conflicting objectives but realize mutual benefit can be gained by agreement, even if the grounds on which such agreement is made differ from their original position.

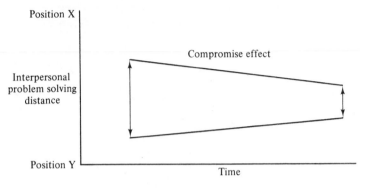

Fig. 10.5

Let us consider the case incident of the representatives of management and employees discussing the wage claim. In the example, neither side was prepared to give ground. If, however, they were prepared to compromise, the discussion might develop in the following way:

MANAGEMENT REPRESENTATIVE: If your members insist on a 10 per cent claim at this time, the economic future for the company is dismal. It is essential that some of the profits are ploughed back as investment to create more work and jobs. If we don't do this, we may have to declare redundancies.

EMPLOYEE REPRESENTATIVE: It's no use trying to scare us into withdrawing our claim by hypothetical predictions. We still have a short-term problem that the employees feel that 5 per cent is not adequate to cover their needs.

MANAGEMENT REPRESENTATIVE: We understand this problem. Likewise our major problem is to increase productivity at a lower unit cost. We would be willing to increase the wage offer to 7 per cent, if your members would guarantee to operate in full the proposals on manning discussed last year and increase productivity by 5 per cent.

EMPLOYEE REPRESENTATIVE: This seems to be a possible answer, provided the company is willing to come forward with the remaining 3 per cent of our claim within six months if the employees exceed the productivity requirement.

MANAGEMENT REPRESENTATIVE: We would agree to this.

Here, the parties in the discussion are negotiating a solution. Neither side obtained exactly what it required, but each gained something. A compromise solution emerged with both sides moving from their original position to agree to a solution that they both feel will be acceptable. At the end of the meeting, both decide to review the solution within a specified time.

CONVERSATIONAL DISTANCE
As shown in the above examples, the distance between people can increase, remain the same, or be reduced during a discussion. The four conversational effects outlined above illustrate the way discussions can move. If, for example, each side disagrees or rejects ideas from the other side, then the distance between them will widen. Where one party is prepared to agree or commit himself to a proposal of the other, the distance between them will narrow as the persuasion effect occurs. Where both parties are committed to their own point of view exclusively, even after consideration of the other's position, then stalemate is reached. Finally, if both parties are prepared to give ground for advantages offered, then it is likely that the distance between them will decrease, even though both move further away from their original objective. It is vital in any discussion to know whether the distance between yourself and the other party is increasing or decreasing in order to assess whether or not you are having the intended effect.

Responses Influencing IPS Distance
The above effects are those which are most common, although others do occur. The central question that needs to be resolved is to identify the responses people make in problem-solving situations that are likely to produce these types of effects. Consider the responses a person could make in an interpersonal problem-solving situation. To what extent is each response likely to bring about agreement or disagreement?

One of your staff comes and informs you that his machine has broken down and requires attention. These are some of the possible responses:

Accusation: 'No wonder it's broken down, you never spend any time servicing it. It's you that is to blame, not the machine.'

Suggestion: 'Why don't you ask Tom to have a look at it for you?'

Apologise: 'Sorry, but I haven't got time to fix it.'

Punish: 'Your machine is always breaking down. I'm going to take you off that job and put you back on unskilled work.'

Help: 'Let me have a go at fixing it.'

Consultative Support: 'Where is the fault?'

Consultative Attack: 'Why is it always your machine that breaks down?'

Bargain: 'If we can get the machine going, I'll make it worth your while to stay on tonight and finish the job.'

Command: 'Get someone to mend the machine immediately.'

Threat: 'If that machine is not in working order within the hour, I'll get someone else to do the job!'

Listen: 'Tell me more, you say the machine is broken?'

These are just a few approaches, and each would produce a somewhat different response from the person presenting the problem. Some of the responses create tension and produce conflict, others lead towards problem diagnosis, and some towards the generation of solutions.

Again, there is no one best answer. It may be that you, as the manager in this case, knowing the man involved, his work record, and various other factors, would wish to verbally attack him and raise interpersonal tension. On the one hand, in your judgement, this might be the best way to jolt the man towards solving the problem and improving performance. On the other, you may judge that the best approach is to lower the tension and develop a dialogue on how best to solve the problem.

The crucial point is, will heightening the tension by verbally attacking the man motivate him to resolve the problem? It may also have an effect on your interpersonal relations, which could make interpersonal problem solving in the future more difficult. For example, the man may seek to conceal errors and defects in the future, rather than discuss them with you. The essential question that must be asked is, will your response reduce or widen the distance between you and the other person?

ESTABLISHING PROBLEM-SOLVING CONDITIONS

Interpersonal problem solving can only succeed if the parties feel capable of expressing their views. If people feel constrained, they will guard what they say to such an extent that aspects of the problem may not come to light, and when solutions are sought possible contributions will be suppressed.

In essence, successful interpersonal problem solving depends substantially on the extent to which you feel you can trust the other person. Will he scorn your problem? Will he blame you? Will he ignore or play down your concern? Will he attack you for causing the problem? Alternatively, will the person to whom you are presenting the problem listen, encourage you, advise, share the problem, help you think, and enable you to learn new ways of tackling the problem?

Most people prefer to present a problem to a person who engages in the latter form of behaviour. Intuitively, we judge what we say to a person in an interpersonal problem-solving situation according to whether we think he will be helpful, considerate, understanding, hostile, or apathetic to whatever is of concern to us.

Managers have often been heard to say during a dispute that their door was always open for anyone to come and see them, but no one ever did. The conclusion could be that those involved in the dispute did not perceive the manager as a person with whom a problem could be discussed.

To create a climate within which interpersonal problem solving can improve, the senior manager in any unit must take a lead in creating an atmosphere in which people can talk meaningfully to one another. This involves listening to what people mean, as opposed to what they say. It involves being helpful in a practical manner, rather than just being sympathetic. It means an orientation towards developing people, rather than depressing them with guilt and blame for causing problems. It involves the mutual sharing of views and facts pertaining to common work problems. Above all, it involves facilitating improved ways in which people relate with one another in accomplishing a particular task.

Conclusion

As yet we are only beginning to understand what 'turns people off', what 'turns people on', what makes people angry, and what brings about mutual problem-solving behaviour. One thing however is certain, we tend to respond not only to what another person says, but the manner or tone in which he says it. It is, therefore, in the way we verbally communicate that we must primarily assess the means for improving behaviour. This chapter has outlined some of the aspects of this subject.

Summary

A. In this chapter, attention has been drawn to behavioural aspects of decision making in which a consideration of the following issues has taken place:
- Interpersonal problem-solving distance.
- Conversational decision responses.
- Types of discussion.
- Conversational distance.
- Developing an interpersonal problem-solving climate.
B. In particular, the chapter should enable the manager to:
- Assess the range of conversational responses in problem solving.
- Identify the major types of discussion.
- Recognize the reduction or expansion of conversational distance.
- Understand the importance of developing an appropriate problem-solving climate.
C. In considering the issues raised, a manager should ask himself:
- What sort of discussions do I have, and with whom?
- What behaviour occurs in the successful and unsuccessful meetings I attend?
- What should I do to further effective behavioural relationships for problem solving?

11

SOCIAL DISTANCE AND PROBLEM SOLVING

'I've got a lot of time for Jack Ford,' said Bill Dodson, production manager at the ACW Car Co., 'he's always been most helpful to me on problems that have required some computer work.'

'Well, that surprises me,' replied Dave Reynolds, the firm's chief accountant. 'As far as I'm concerned, he just makes my life one big headache. He's always around asking awkward questions, and when I want to know something in return he says it will have to wait until he's programmed his machines. I'm not at all sure he's really up to the job.'

'Well, there's no doubt in my mind,' replied Dodson. 'I agree he takes time to get things set up, but he really knows what he's doing. He has cut my work down by about 20 to 30 per cent. I really admire his ability to sort out difficult problems. He is one of the few people in this place I feel I can look up to.'

'Perhaps I haven't given him a fair chance,' replied Reynolds. 'Our personalities are not exactly complementary. In fact, up to now, I've always tended to pay scant attention to his operations. If anything, I've regarded him and his group as the poor relation of commercial administration.'

STATUS DIFFERENTIALS

Clearly, these are two very different views of one man and his job. Within the work situation, most of us tend to look at our associates and make judgements about their position, their work, their personalities, their ideas, and a host of other things. The result is that we develop a scale of values on which subjectively we place ourselves in relation to others. This we shall call the *status differential*.

People acquire status in the eyes of others by doing or having various things. For example, doctors in our society tend to have high status because of their specialized knowledge and ability to deal with illness. Traditionally, priests have had high status, along with lawyers, teachers, and military people. Today, the status positions may be changing as scientists, businessmen, computer technologists, entertainment artistes, and others develop their skills.

However, within each organization there is also a status hierarchy in which people judge the weight and worth of other functions and individuals. This process of judging the status of others is important in the problem-solving process and we shall seek to examine it further, in terms of 'looking down', 'looking across', or 'looking upward' at people.

The Status Differential Scale

It is possible to examine the way people judge others on the scale shown in Fig. 11.1.

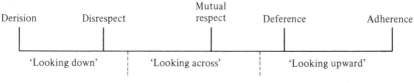

Fig. 11.1

Within this scale, the terms can be defined in the following way.

Derision If a person has a very low opinion of another person, or his views, then he has the behavioural alternative of acting in a derisive manner towards that person. This will involve behaviour such as ignoring his comments; saying his remarks are irrelevant; calling him abusive names; undermining his position; depriving him of resources and opportunities; and scorning his attitudes, ideas, skills, and behaviour, to the extent of deliberately acting in a manner contrary to that which the other would wish.

Disrespect This is another form of making a judgement on another which implies that one is disapproving and 'looking down' on him. It involves behaviours similar to those described above, but they are not as severe in tone. Disrespect will involve behaviour that puts another 'in his place' by contradicting him; being sarcastic; treating him in a non-adult manner; rejecting his arguments without reason; overriding his objection to proposals; deferring his requests without cause; refusing to listen to his communications; and indicating to him that he does not have as much power, prestige, and influence as you and others.

Mutual Respect This is a situation where there is a relationship between two (or more) people that is seen to have advantages to both parties. Each party has something that the other values. They, therefore, have a mutual respect for each other based on their admiration of their respective abilities, wealth, position, knowledge, or whatever is the common currency. They will grant 'favours' to each other; provide time to meet each other; and endeavour to maintain the basis for mutual respect. Although mutual respect is based on some form of exchange, it does not need to be material in form. Mutual respect can be based on humour, beauty, honesty, beliefs, and other factors. The important point is that both parties treat each other as equals. Although they may act in a competitive manner from time to time, they do so with due regard to each other's strengths.

Deference   When one party in a relationship feels the other has more knowledge, experience, authority, resources, or ability, then it is possible that the former will defer to the judgement of the latter on various issues. Deference involves an acknowledgement that the other party has some prior claim on the situation. If one defers to another, it is implied that he is invited to take the lead. To this end, leadership is linked with the willingness of the followers to go along with the initiatives of the leader. Deference, therefore, involves 'looking up' to someone; seeking out his opinion; granting him time and effort; being prepared to listen willingly to his ideas; being predisposed to his beliefs; supporting his initiatives; allowing his plans precedence over your own; following rather than leading.

Adherence   This is a relationship where one person or party accepts the views and initiatives of the other and acts upon them. Adherence involves obedience. In this relationship, one person does not question the other for he is the authority. The structure of the armed forces includes this sort of relationship, based upon respect for rank. People below a given rank are expected to 'look up' with respect to their superiors and obey their commands. Adherence goes beyond deference, in so far as one party is expected to comply rather than merely acknowledge the other's superiority. It involves a near-total commitment, not out of necessity, but a belief that the system, the rank, and therefore the person who makes decisions, are the best that can be achieved in the situation, and should be respected and willingly obeyed.

SOCIAL DISTANCE

In the initial example, Dodson and Reynolds had differing views on the computer man, Jack Ford. Dodson felt that on technical matters he would certainly have mutual respect, if not deference, for Ford's ability and contribution to his own work. Reynolds during the conversation showed that, if anything, he had disrespect for Ford and his work, although so far this had not reached the stage of derision.

These judgements reflect a social distance. Just as one can be geographically distant from another, so it is possible to have a social distance between yourself and others. It is reflected in the number of times one talks to another; the manner or tone of the conversation; the extent to which one undermines the other's position; or fails to listen, help, share, and communicate. Where there is mutual respect there may still be social distance – for it may be respect born out of fear. However, in most cases, social distance is smallest where mutual respect exists and is greatest where derision or adherence exist. But in all relationships social distance exists in some measure and has an effect on the problem-solving process.

Social distance based on the status differential is not a constant phenomenon. For example, it is possible to have deference for a person's ability at golf, but disrespect for his ability at work. In making a total judgement about a person, we tend to weigh a number of factors together.

Social Distance and Role Relations

Within the work situation, managers have a number of different types of role relationship with others as identified in the model in Fig. 11.2.

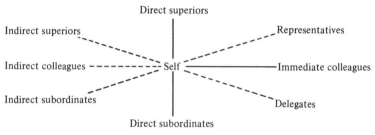

Fig. 11.2   Role relationships

The continuous black lines in the model refer to relationships where a formal organizational link exists between you and another person. For example, your direct superior will probably control your salary, resources, opportunities within the organization, and work load. Likewise, these areas will probably be those where you exercise influence over your direct subordinates. With immediate colleagues the relationship may be more complex, but will involve the same factors. The broken lines refer to relationships where you either have influence, or are influenced, but on more informal lines.

In all these relationships, there is a tendency to make status judgements. We gain impressions of others and put them on a scale of approachability. How interesting are these people? How easy to talk to? How influential are they? What will happen if we tell the other person what we know? Is it worth while trying to get the other person to act? Has he the position to do anything to help? These are just some of the questions that we often ask ourselves when confronted by a work problem.

Let us take the case of Dodson and Reynolds again to illustrate the same aspects of social distance and problem solving.

DODSON: This man Ford is, in my view, only the beginning of a number of big changes in this company that will affect old-timers like you and me.

REYNOLDS: I'm not sure. I've just spent the morning looking at the work of the three new people I took on last year. They are all graduates, but they know little about the practical aspects of accountancy.

DODSON: But they learn fast. I've got a few of these university blokes in my department. When they arrived they were all theory, but they picked up the basics in a short time.

REYNOLDS: It's this theory stuff that is the trouble. I don't understand what they are talking about, and what's more I'm not sure they do. They speak a different language to people like us. What I want is someone with bags of experience and his feet on the floor.

DODSON: I agree that some of them are difficult to understand, but I think we have got to make the effort. Take this new director who's just been appointed. He has degrees from a business school, but not as much experience as either of us. However, he is a most interesting person to talk to on business problems. I had lunch with him yesterday and he told me how decision theory could make my unit more effective. We've decided to set up a project on it and work closely together. I think this decision theory could be useful to your area as well.

REYNOLDS: That may be, but why change something that's working satisfactorily? I've met this new bloke at a committee meeting. He asked a lot of questions, but didn't seem to have any answers. Talking to people like that worries me. I like to know what people are thinking. The one thing I like about my boss, the finance director, is that he sets things out in black and white. He tells me when a job must be finished and it's my task to get it done. He doesn't question my methods. He is interested in results.

DODSON: I agree that bosses shouldn't interfere in the doing of the job, but new methods are vital if we are going to remain efficient. I make it a part of my job to meet as many people as possible and find out what they do and how it can help me in my job. The people I don't like are those who are not interested in sharing their ideas.

REYNOLDS: Well that's the main problem round here. People won't cooperate. Half my time is spent chasing people in marketing and sales, trying to get figures from them. They are not prepared to help. Yet they complain when my department doesn't produce their expense claims on time.

This conversation is designed deliberately to illustrate the difference between a person who is seeking to reduce social distance between himself and others, and the person who widens the social distance. In essence, Dodson is always looking towards others in a collaborative manner. He is willing to learn and respect the new people, recognizing the contribution they can make. Reynolds, in contrast, is sceptical and suspicious. He has little trust in them and sees their contribution to the organization as a potential threat to his own work. He, therefore, seeks to 'look down' upon their efforts, and derides them for not having sufficient experience: being too theoretical; not speaking in normal language; and trying to change well-established procedures. Accordingly, he finds reasons why he should not discuss matters with them and voices his disrespect. At the same time, he is concerned that they may have some valuable ideas that he won't be able to understand or use, and they will as a consequence disrespect him.

The result in terms of problem solving can be significant. Dodson is open-minded and 'looks across' and 'looks up' at people for ideas and information. He wishes to reduce the social distance between himself and others, regardless if the person is a subordinate or a superior. His concern is to gain information to help him cope with the problems of managing his department.

Reynolds is close-minded, which is likely to widen the distance between himself and others. Even with his own superior, he maintains a relationship at arm's length. By making negative status judgements about others, Reynolds indicates his unwillingness to meet the new people, to share his views with them, to listen, and to learn. He has consequently begun to increase the social distance between himself and others, and at the same time reduce his access to problem-solving information and resources.

STATUS RELATIONS IN CONVERSATION

The impact of status judgements are felt most profoundly during a conversation when one person makes a judgement about another's work, position, or ability that implies a status differential. Take, for example, another case incident between executives at a managerial meeting:

CHAIRMAN: We must now consider when we are going ahead with our new product.

MARKETING MANAGER: We are now in a position to launch the new product. We have done all our field tests. The reports indicate we would sell the required number in the set price range. It is important that we get the product to the market within the next six weeks.

RESEARCH MANAGER: That is easier said than done. Your marketing survey has shown that we need to look more closely at the fluidity of the mixture in the product. This will take us another three or four weeks.

PRODUCTION MANAGER: I wish you two people could make up your minds. I am all geared up for production, but as yet there is no product. I've got people and machines standing idle. If you people were made to do some firm planning, like we have to do, we wouldn't get into a situation like this.

MARKETING MANAGER: Well it's not our fault. We have done our tests. What we need now is some action, otherwise we will be advertising a product which is not for sale.

RESEARCH MANAGER: That is the trouble with you marketing people – you are in too much of a hurry. It's easy to do a market survey, but we have to deal with the results. You can't rush research work in the same slap-happy way you tackle market surveys.

MARKETING MANAGER: Look, we do a thorough job. I accept that the survey has suggested slight changes in the mixture composition. I don't know enough about your job to contradict your view that it takes two weeks or more to do this.

PRODUCTION MANAGER: While you two are arguing, my department is standing idle with the costs rising. It's about time you got it sorted out and let me have a definite date for production.

In this meeting, a problem exists which is exacerbated by the various managers making status judgements about their own and other departments' functions. The production man is accusing the other two of upsetting his schedules, raising his costs, and creating man–management problems. The research manager deflates the work of the marketing function by suggesting it is easier to do a market survey than a research test. The marketing manager feels he is being held back by the research manager, but defers to the latter's superior knowledge on how long changes will take.

The members of the group are creating social distance between themselves, by making judgements about each other's work. Most of the comments imply disrespect of the others' attitudes and work. There is little concern for the problems of the other, and little attempt to reach a mutually agreeable solution. The problem-solving process is not moving forward, as those involved are more concerned to defend themselves and their job. Most people have taken up either defensive or aggressive positions. The chairman recognizes the dilemma and intervenes to reduce social distance and improve the problem-solving process:

CHAIRMAN: We are losing sight of the real problem, which is when can we market this new product? At the moment, we are busy scoring points off each other, and defending our work interests. What we need to do is consider the timetable for the launch. I want you to tell me how long it will take to complete the work to be done.

RESEARCH MANAGER: It will take me two weeks to finish, if we work flat out.

MARKETING MANAGER: The advertising material is now ready for printing and can be available in two weeks.

PRODUCTION MANAGER: We need to have some trial runs, but could probably do this in the next two weeks while the tests are going on. After that we should have sufficient quantities to put on the market three weeks from the time of starting full production, provided we work weekends and evenings. This will mean taking on extra labour, say, for about a month.

CHAIRMAN: Well, it looks as if we could be operational in five weeks. Let us proceed on that plan. In the meantime, I want to know immediately if there is any delay in your areas. We shall then have an emergency meeting to decide on the issues.

Here, the chairman redirects the meeting away from interpersonal status judgements to the problem situation. He emphasizes the need for the executives to have mutual respect for each other's work and time targets. Furthermore, he emphasizes the necessity to maintain close social distance, should delays occur, rather than argue over whose fault they were or who has the most difficult task.

Conclusion

This chapter has outlined some of the issues in the relationships between people in problem solving. It has concentrated on the effect of making social status judgements. Whenever we meet another person, we tend intuitively to rank him as, for example, clever, shy, honest, sharp, slow, intelligent, helpful, or unfair. In making such judgements, we are likely to say to ourselves that he is either 'a person worth listening to', or 'someone who should go far', or 'a person who doesn't know what he is talking about'. This sort of judgement process, it is suggested, can be looked at on a status differential scale.

If we accept this analysis, then it can be said that people's relations with us are based on 'looking down', 'looking across', or 'looking up' to us. When, during meetings, these attitudes are communicated from one person to another, social distance can either be increased or reduced. It is suggested that in most cases the problem-solving process is likely to be facilitated when the social distance between people is reduced to a point where they have mutual respect for each other's contributions.

Summary

A. In this chapter, attention has been drawn to:
- The relationship of status, social distance, and problem solving.
- Status differentials.
- The measurement of status.
- Status relations in organizations and conversations.

B. In particular, the chapter should enable the manager to:
- Identify comments implying differential status.
- Gauge the status relationships between people in conversation.
- Assess the relationship between social distance and problem solving.
- Develop an awareness of status judgements that facilitate and impede problem solving.

C. In considering the issues raised in this chapter, the manager should ask himself:
- With whom do I relate most easily, and why?
- Whom do I 'look down' upon, and 'look up' to?
- Do these people reciprocate in a similar manner?
- Which tasks and functions do I have high and low respect for?
- What do I need to do to become more effective in this area of interpersonal problem solving?

12

PUNISHMENT

Most of us are very adept at dealing out a kind of punishment. It is not always immediately recognizable, for it does not involve physical injury. It is a much more subtle form which concentrates on attacking people's feelings, beliefs, and activities. The main weapons are words and gestures, and they serve to widen the social distance between people.

Take George Taylor, for example. He rushed out of his office one morning to a meeting. As he went, he handed his secretary some papers and asked her to type them out. The meeting lasted all morning and was followed by a business lunch. Taylor arrived back at his office at 2.30 PM. He hurried into his secretary's room: 'I need those papers I gave you this morning', he said. 'They are not typed yet,' she replied. 'I thought that you could have managed that by now,' said Taylor.

The punishment has begun. Taylor may or may not be justified. His secretary may have been slow. The point is, should Taylor have said the last sentence? It implies that his secretary has failed in his eyes. She has not lived up to his expectations and he responds by indicating clearly that he feels she has let him down. He has begun to attribute blame.

It is not an uncommon occurrence. Some people would hardly regard it as a harsh punishment. But, clearly, Taylor is not giving the girl praise. He could, of course, have made the punishment more severe by saying, 'I thought that *even you* could have managed that by now'. This highlights the attack in so far as it brings in a comparative dimension. Moreover, it is an invidious comparison, as the force of the comment 'even you' implies that at the best of times the girl's performance is poor.

Let us return to Taylor's original comment. What was he trying to achieve? Initially, he was giving vent to his feelings. He had another meeting to attend and required the papers urgently. His comment was one of anger. However, what effect would it have on the secretary? How could she respond?

POSSIBLE RESPONSES TO PUNISHMENT

The secretary could reply in any of the following ways:
1. 'I'm sorry, I'll do it immediately.'
    or
2. 'I didn't realize that you wanted the papers this afternoon.'
    or
3. 'I can't do everything at once.'
    or
4. 'I've had enough of this pressure, I can't go on.'
    or
5. 'It's your fault, you should have told me you wanted them this afternoon.'

Behavioural Responses

If the secretary adopts response 1, she is being *supportive*. Her concern is to get the job done rather than have an argument. The fact that she says she's sorry may mean she feels that the punishment is deserved. If, for example, the papers were required each week at the same time, then she might well feel that it was her fault. But does the secretary really feel sorry? Is this a polite way of dealing with the punishment when really she feels anger at Taylor's comment? This may emerge in the long run, but the first response is to support Taylor by offering to do the job.

Response 2 is a *defensive* reaction. The secretary pleads ignorance of the fact the papers were required, and therefore suggests she is not to be blamed. She thereby seeks to protect her position without making any evaluative comments about the situation. Again, she may be angry with Taylor's remark but does not say so. On the other hand, she may feel it was made in a non-vindictive manner.

Response 3 is a similar form of reply, but is essentially *fixative*. The girl is not adding anything to her original statement that the papers are not ready. She is beginning to say the same thing in different words. There is a note of defeat in her comment, and she may feel she does not know what to do next. This is the beginning of a fixative situation, where a person begins to go round in circles on a problem.

Response 4 does involve movement. The girl cracks under the punishing comment and her reply is a *regressive* one. In effect, she says she is with-

drawing from the job. She refers to the 'pressure' which
or Taylor's punishing comments. The result, howeve.
indicates she is not prepared to continue.

Response 5 is *aggressive*. It is a counter-attack to
ment. The secretary here feels that she is being blamed unjus
erefore responds by laying the blame with Taylor for not infor
of the urgency of the job. In effect, the secretary responds by se
punish Taylor for creating the situation.

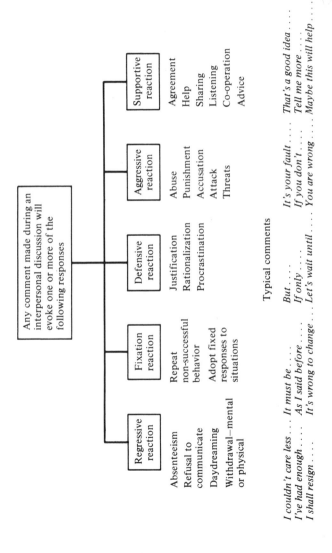

Fig. 12.1 Interpersonal reaction and responses

FORMS OF PUNISHMENT

These responses are examples of the ways in which a person can react when confronted by a situation where another accuses, blames, or induces guilt. The nature of verbal punishment has many varieties. The following examples illustrate some of the many ways in which a person can try to downgrade, depress, or undermine another.

Sarcasm

In a way, sarcasm exaggerates the offence that is being punished. For the purpose of example, we shall stay with our mythical manager George Taylor. When he went to his first meeting, his aim was to try and increase his advertising budget as sales in his area were falling. When it came to his turn to speak, he said that sales were down because competitors were spending more on publicity and that a further £10 000 for advertising should improve the situation. His colleagues at the meeting were surprised and felt his claim was out of proportion to the other requirements, such as new plant and research expenditure.

One of his colleagues looked at him and said, 'Have you tried halving the price of the product?' Another asked rhetorically, 'Are you sure £10 000 isn't cutting it a bit fine?'

Sarcasm is a form of punishment that attacks the person or subject obliquely. It is designed to deflate this speaker by seeming to take his original statement at face value, but adding a comment that calls into question the seriousness of the proposal. Sarcasm therefore is a form of punishment that belittles the thought process of the other person and thereby attacks the substance of a proposal.

Implication

This again is an indirect form of punishment. Someone may say to George Taylor in the meeting: 'What is required is an analysis of the whole marketing operation. What happens to all the money we spend on advertising at present? We could be throwing good money after bad.'

This speaker throws doubt on the existing management of the sales expenditure and implies that things are not what they should be. He asks for information, but this can be read as an indirect attack on the way Taylor is operating. A stronger version of this approach is used by the man who says: 'I'm surprised you are asking for more money, George. I would have thought you had more than enough to do the job.'

Blame

This is a direct form of punishment. The person who attributes blame feels he knows the cause of a problem and, moreover, feels the need to allocate the blame to a person. As one of Taylor's colleagues said, 'The trouble is, George, you have run out of money because you overspent on that mail order promotion. It seems to me you could have saved a lot there.' This is a direct and specific attack, unlike the previous forms, which were based on innuendo.

Blame is a powerful weapon of punishment. Whenever something goes wrong, we tend to look for a culprit. Who caused the trouble? He must be taken to task. We do this often when the lesson has been well learned by the person who is responsible for the mistake. For example, if someone dropped a piece of equipment, we might say 'You wouldn't have done that if you were keeping your eye on the job', when it is quite clear to the person in question that this was the cause of the mishap. The comment only adds insult to the injury.

Accusation

This form of punishment is close to blame. It differs in the extent to which the person who is giving the punishment knows the cause of the offence. In order to establish guilt, an accusation is made. At this point, a person has to accept or deny the allegation. Accusations are often made when there is insufficient evidence for blame, but sufficient suspicion to allow for the former. The fact that somebody is accused of an error is in itself a punishment. George Taylor, for example, was accused during the meeting by one of his colleagues of falsifying the figures by bringing non-recurrent expenditure into account. This was an allegation that required discussion, but the very fact that such an allegation was made was in itself a form of verbal punishment.

Attribution

The distinction between attribution, accusation, and blame is again cloudy, but sufficient in itself to provide a different form of verbal punishment. Attribution involves making reference to another person or his possessions in an evaluative manner. Where this is done in a way that downgrades, punishment has occurred.

George Taylor felt he had to make a stand against the attacks on his proposal for more money. He did so by trying his own attack and thereby punishing the other members of the group. 'The point I am making,' he began, 'is that this company lives or dies on the sales it makes. I recognize the claims of others, but they are not as urgent as the one I am making. Your programmes are less critical. Your trouble is that you are too concerned with production. You need to be outward-looking.'

Here, Taylor responds by punishing his colleagues through attributing to them a series of comments about the priority of their work and their narrow view of the business. In this case, Taylor clearly means his comments to be adversely critical.

There are other occasions where attribution is used to praise people, when, for example, one person says to another 'You are much better at doing that job than I am'. In this case, a favourable judgement of the other person has been made. It is when an unfavourable judgement is made during the process of attribution that punishment occurs.

DEALING WITH ERRORS

Can one avoid verbally punishing another person? Consider that you have asked one of your subordinates to bring you a report. His task was to assess the areas for sales expansion. You receive the report two days late. It is poorly written with many spelling errors. The structure of the report is not clear and no index or synopsis is provided. Finally, the report only covers half the areas you had expected information upon. The subordinate comes to see you and says he found 'it difficult to get the report done in the time'.

Let us take this example as the basis for comparing two different approaches to dealing with the situation. One approach we shall refer to as *punishment-centred*, the other as *problem-solving*.

For the purpose of the comparison, we shall examine possible replies that people might make, using the five managerial problem-solving approaches:

1. Reflective
2. Consultative
3. Negotiative
4. Prescriptive
5. Directive.

Each of these approaches is illustrated in terms of a punishment-centred response, compared to a problem-solving approach.

	PUNISHMENT-CENTRED APPROACH	PROBLEM-SOLVING APPROACH
Reflective:	You mean to say that two weeks wasn't sufficient time to get this job done?	You felt you didn't have enough time?
Consultative:	What have you been doing with your time? The report is two days late already. There must be some explanation?	Tell me, what problems did you encounter in doing the report?
Negotiative:	Take the report away and let me have it completed by the weekend or else I will take you off this sort of work. This is your last chance.	I have indicated on the report where it requires attention. Let me have it back by the weekend in good shape and I shall put you in for the salary rise you asked for.
Prescriptive:	You can do better than this. If I were you, I would go through it again, carefully,	I would like to see the report written more clearly and expanded to cover other areas.

	and expand it. Perhaps you could try this time to have it in on time?	Why don't you spend a couple of days on it and let me see it at the weekend?
Directive:	This report is poor. It's just not up to standard. I want it done again. This time, correct the grammar, give a synopsis and index. Also expand the area of coverage. I don't want any excuses this time. We are not running a charity. I want it on my desk by Friday.	The report needs changing on things like grammar and spelling. Put in a synopsis and index. Widen the coverage. I want the report completed and on my desk by Friday.

The punishment-centred approach involves the use of adjectives to emphasize the nature of the response. These adjectives are negative and critical rather than positive in the sense of praise. The responses are designed not only to convey a message about the task, but to attack the individual and his performance.

The problem-solving responses are also critical in so far as they indicate that the performance is not adequate. However, a central difference is that they do not make a personal attack on the individual. The focus of the response is the task, not the person. Either questions are asked about the problems involved, or solutions indicating what is required.

In short, the *punishment-centred response* highlights the failings of the *individual* and upbraids his performance. The focus is on criticizing the person. The *problem-solving approach* stresses the *task*, the *problem*, the *situation*, and the requirements necessary to achieve the *objective*.

WHAT IS PUNISHMENT MEANT TO ACHIEVE?

Whenever we make a comment about someone else's behaviour we are in fact saying to him or her:

- 'Do more of it.'
- 'Keep doing it as at present.'
- 'Do less of it.'
- 'Stop doing it.'

Thus, when we make an evaluative comment to a person, which we have referred to here as punishment, what is our objective? Basically, there are three possible alternatives.

1. Reformation

We may criticize another person with a view to shaming him into changing his behaviour. When, for example, we say 'That's a stupid thing to do' or 'Don't you realize that as a result of your doing that . . . ?', we may really want to ensure that the person does not repeat the behaviour. We try to reach our objective by attacking what we feel he has done wrong.

However, this does not necessarily lead to an improvement or reform. To punish what has occurred may not help the person to change. Suppose the manager had confronted the subordinate who did the poor report and said, 'I'm not happy with that report. There are lots of mistakes in it. You must be more careful. You don't seem to have your mind on the job. Now I want the report done again and this time make sure it's right.' Would this help improve the situation?

The manager has indicated that he is dissatisfied and verbally punishes the individual. However, he does not help him correct his errors. The manager offers no guidance as to what must be done to meet his standards. He concentrates on the negative rather than the positive side. In most cases, this will not bring about an improvement. The individual concerned will be in even more difficulty, trying to understand what is required.

If the aim of punishment is reform, then not only must the errors be pointed out and eradicated, but positive guidance needs to be offered as to how to improve. In sporting terms, it's little use telling a person he is playing the wrong shot, say, at cricket or golf, if you do not give guidance on what is a correct shot.

Verbal punishment, therefore, may be useful as a means of helping extinguish undesired behaviour if it is also associated with constructive help. This, of course, assumes that the individual concerned:

- Wants to extinguish a given pattern of behaviour.
- Is receptive to verbal punishment as a means of helping to extinguish a pattern of behaviour.

In most cases, verbal punishment is not useful as a means of reform. However, criticizing people may motivate them to do better if:

- They accept they have failed.
- Feel the need to change their behaviour.
- Have a regard and confidence in the critic.

Even so, the criticism will not be sufficient where it is necessary to change a person's skill to do a job. The manager in the case above may change the subordinate's attitude to the job through verbal punishment. However, if the subordinate does not possess the necessary writing and research skills, he will never produce a good report, regardless of his effort.

Reformation is more likely to be influenced by praise rather than punishment, but even this has limitations. The most important thing is for the individual to want to achieve a standard and have the opportunity to acquire the skills necessary to do the job. Punishment only goes part of the way. It attacks attitudes – which may, of course, be strengthened, not weakened, by the attack – rather than changes people's abilities.

2. Retribution

People often verbally punish others to 'even up the score', as the phrase goes. Retribution involves the concept of 'an eye for an eye and a tooth for a tooth'. Therefore, if someone verbally attacks you, there is usually a strong tendency to reply in kind. Conversations take place such as the following:

MANAGER: That report is just not good enough. What have you been doing with your time? Your trouble is you spend too much time talking and not enough working.

SUBORDINATE: That's unfair. I work as hard as the others around here. My problem is that you are hardly ever here to sort out the problems. You don't even give clear instructions on what should be done. It's no use you trying to pass the blame on to me. If I spend a lot of time talking, it's only trying to clarify the mess you have created.

Here the subordinate fears he is being criticized unjustly and begins to trade verbal blows with his boss. His long-term aim may be to get his boss to change. In the short run, however, he is defending himself by criticizing his boss in a manner similar to the one in which he was attacked. If nothing more occurs, the subordinate will feel that he has tried to give as good as he received. Where this happens, there is a tendency for both parties to start defending their own position and attacking the other individual. This usually results in behaviour whereby one person tries to gain a point at the expense of the other. This is hardly conducive to problem solving.

3. Restitution

This involves making amends. Punishment usually occurs when one person perceives another to have acted in a manner contrary to his standards or desires. If both parties agree that an error has been committed, it is normal for the offending party to make restitution in the same way. Very often we say 'I am sorry for the inconvenience I have caused', or make some other verbal apology. However, where a person recognizes he is in error, but gets severely and verbally punished, he will find it difficult to make restitution.

Making restitution is a very important part of problem solving. It is a common occurrence for misunderstanding in conversation. The speaker has two choices. He can blame the other person, by saying: 'No, you got that wrong. I didn't say that. You haven't understood what I was saying.' Alternatively, the speaker can say: 'I'm sorry, I must have not made that clear. The point I was concerned about was . . . .' Here the speaker puts the blame upon himself rather than punishing the other person. In doing so, he makes restitution for an error in communication, regardless of whether the speaker was to blame.

Restitution may not necessarily mean admitting liability and blame. It also involves a person gaining recompense for injury. This is not just 'an eye for an eye', but a more positive claim to compensate for injury sustained. As indicated, it can be that a person asks for and receives an apology. Restitution may go beyond the verbal level and be achieved by monetary payment, as, for example, in pending civil court actions settled outside court. The restitution of verbal punishment can take many forms, but the most common verbal restitutions are the apology, the explanation, and the acceptance of points made by others.

PUNISHMENT AVOIDANCE

Naturally, most people seek to avoid punishment. Therefore, in an environment where people expect to be punished, all sorts of avoidance tactics are worked out. It is a well known caricature that the civil servant sends numerous copies of memoranda to various people not just for information, but to 'cover himself' against contingency.

Where mistakes do occur people develop a variety of techniques for avoiding blame. Let us look at an example. An operative working overtime was assembling a piece of machinery which was later found to have certain wrong components. The inspector told the operative's foreman who spoke to the operative about it:

FOREMAN: I've just had a message from the inspector about that job you did last night. He says it's all wrong. There were parts used which were for the ARB version. Now, you knew that last night you were doing a special job on the ARB 2 machine. How come you made the mistake? It will cost us a lot of money . . . .

OPERATIVE: Don't blame me. No one told me I was supposed to be working on the ARB 2. I just followed the plan I had and used the materials provided.

FOREMAN: I can't believe that! I know I was away yesterday and didn't give out the overtime. Who told you to do the job?

OPERATIVE: The general foreman came round and asked me to work over and get out a special order. I agreed and I'm not taking the blame if things have gone wrong.

FOREMAN: They've gone wrong all right. That special order was urgent. We may even lose the customer, never mind the cost of putting the job right.

The foreman is in a difficult position. The operative has evaded responsibility for the error. He argues that he was not aware that he had to work on the ARB 2. However, if that is true, and the foreman is suspicious that it is not, what should he do? Can he go to his boss, the general foreman, and blame him? This is more difficult than approaching and blaming an operative. The foreman, therefore, changes his strategy:

FOREMAN: I've had a word about this mess up on the ARB 2 job.
                    The operative says he didn't know that he had to
                    assemble the ARB 2.
GENERAL FOREMAN: Well his memory must be short. I saw him at four
                    o'clock yesterday and asked him to work over on it.
                    He's just trying to get out of trouble . . . .
FOREMAN: He said he received no new plans and just kept working
                    to the ones he had.
GENERAL FOREMAN: What! He didn't receive the ARB 2 plans? Well, if that's
                    true, no wonder the thing was made up wrongly. I told
                    the planning office to get the ARB 2 plans down to the
                    shop floor by five o'clock last night.

The general foreman begins to feel under pressure. Whose fault is the
error? He agrees to look into the matter with the planning office:

GENERAL FOREMAN: I've come about those plans I asked you to send down
                    to the No. 3 line yesterday evening for the ARB 2 job.
                    The operative says he never received them.
PLANNER: Well, I certainly sent them down.
GENERAL FOREMAN: Where are they now, then?
PLANNER: How do I know? I didn't take them myself.
GENERAL FOREMAN: Who did?
PLANNER: One of the juniors, or maybe my secretary.

The problem of who is to blame gets larger and takes up more time.
The task of discovering who 'failed' becomes more difficult. Each person
has an excuse or explanation which he argues exonerates him from blame.
The whole object of the discussion centres on how to avoid punishment. No
attention is being paid to the question of what can be learned from this experience to help prevent similar occurrences happening again. This trend
continued when the junior draughtsman was questioned:

PLANNER: Did you take the ARB 2 plans down to the assembly shop for
            line No. 3 last night?
JUNIOR: Yes, I took them to the foreman's office for line No. 3. He wasn't
            in, so I left them on his desk.

As the foreman had been away the previous day, the plans were probably
still in the same place. However, numerous other papers had subsequently
been put on the foreman's desk, relegating the plans to the bottom of the
pile. When the foreman came to look through his papers, he found them still
sealed in the envelope in which they were delivered.
    Each person felt he had done his job. But still there was a feeling that

someone should be punished. Who should be the scapegoat? Each person felt it was not his fault, but others in the case might have felt as follows:

1. 'The operative should have known better and looked for the plans before doing the job.'

2. 'The general foreman should have been more specific with his instructions both to the operative and the planner.'

3. 'The planner should have been more precise about his instructions to the junior.'

4. 'The junior should have made sure the plans were handed to a person in the assembly shop rather than leaving them on a desk.'

5. 'The foreman of line No. 3 should have made arrangements in his absence for someone to take responsibility for supervising special work and overtime with whom the general foreman could relate.'

LEARNING FROM FAILURE

If things go wrong, there is usually a tendency to look for the culprit. However, such an approach often leads to avoidance and evasive behaviour. Each person looks for his excuse and alibi.

Where the failure is *accidental*, it is usually more profitable to seek for learning from the events, rather than conduct a punishment-seeking exercise. If the task is rephrased to that of 'identifying what must be done to prevent such errors occurring again', then everyone can contribute ideas. The task is no longer a personal vendetta to identify a scapegoat. The aim is to look at the *situation* with a view to improving the organizational factors influencing performance.

However, when the error is deliberate, it is important to consider whether one should seek to reform, make retribution, or seek verbal restitution. Clearly, if the act was committed deliberately to bring to attention a grievance or a felt injustice, then there is a need for a problem diagnosis. Where the error was committed in a criminal way for gain, then it requires examining within the rules and regulations governing such events.

The distinction between deliberate and accidental error is critical in problem solving. Where an error is dealt with as if it were made with deliberate intent, problem solving will be low; scapegoating will increase, and people will seek to evade punishment. Where the climate differentiates errors, there is the likelihood that people will seek to learn from failure, rather than punish individuals, and restructure the situation to prevent recurrences.

Conclusion: The Importance of Problem Formulation

If the aim is to encourage people to think of ways to improve things, rather than to punish individuals, then the formulation of the presentation is crucial. It is essential to have a problem-centred focus, so that questions are raised to which all parties with knowledge feel they can contribute.

In the previous example, this could have been done by examining 'how to ensure that jobs are done in accordance with the demands of the marketing and production schedule'. Ultimately, the answer could be the simple one employed in most organizations, that no operative starts a job without a job card identifying the precise nature of the job.

However, reaching such a solution may not be easy. If one tackles the problem of 'who to punish', this is a very different task from 'what can we learn from this exercise that will improve our future performance'. In short, it is important to be clear about what objective is being pursued. If it is the latter, then the formulation of the inquiry in a *problem-solving approach*, as identified earlier in the chapter, rather than a *punishment-centred approach*, is more likely to lead to improvements.

Summary

A. In this chapter, attention has been drawn to:
  - The forms of verbal punishment.
  - The alternative behavioural responses.
  - Interpersonal approaches to dealing with errors.
  - The objectives of verbal punishment.
  - The reaction of people to punishment-centred climates.
  - The choice of situational problem solving *versus* personal punishment.
B. In particular, the chapter should enable the manager to:
  - Identify possible approaches for dealing with errors.
  - Distinguish between various verbal punishments.
  - Establish objectives for dealing with interpersonal errors.
  - Choose an interpersonal strategy for dealing with errors.
  - Assess the basis for developing a learning situation.
C. In considering the issues raised, a manager should ask himself:
  - How do I deal with interpersonal errors?
  - When should I seek to verbally punish?
  - What objectives am I pursuing when I engage in such behaviour?
  - How do I convert errors into interpersonal learning situations?

13

HELP: AN ASSESSMENT IN MANAGERIAL PROBLEM SOLVING

MANAGERIAL HELP

How many times have we tried to offer help and had it rejected? Few people keep count of such happenings, but we can all remember an occasion when we have set out with good intentions to help another, but discovered our help has been turned down.

Offering help is an essential part of the managerial problem-solving process. We need, therefore, to consider what are some of the major elements that relate to effective and ineffective help. To do this we shall look at a case example.

John Adams had a problem that had troubled him for over three weeks. It was just three weeks ago that the company he was working for declared 120 men redundant. He had been asked to name two men for redundancy from his department. Sadly, he did so. They were young, unmarried, and not particularly effective at their jobs. They could get employment elsewhere. What worried Adams more was the thought of further redundancies, and particularly what he should do with Bob Parr.

When Adams took over as manager a year ago, there were five supervisors. Bob Parr was one of these. He had been with the company for fifteen years. He was in his middle-thirties and had a wife and four children. He had been made a supervisor two months prior to Adams's arrival. For the last year, he had caused Adams innumerable problems.

Technically, Parr is the best man and produces work of very high calibre. However, he does not supervise his men and seems incapable of doing so. Adams has had to deal with most administrative matters for Parr. The men in Parr's section have no respect for him as a manager. Quality and quantity of output has declined. The men now bypass Parr if they have complaints or a need for help. Adams has spoken to Parr about his supervision, and tried to help but to no avail. The time has come for one last effort before a decision on Parr's future is made, which could lead to him being made redundant.

Adams, therefore, calls Parr in to discuss the matter. ' 'Morning, Bob,' said Adams, 'I've asked you to come over and discuss your job again. Last time you will remember, I asked you to concentrate more on the managerial side of your job. In particular, I wanted you to allocate work evenly and fairly to people, inspect quality and output, help the less experienced members of your section, and organize administrative procedures. How do you feel things have gone?'

Here, Adams summarizes the previous discussion and asks a non-directive question. So far, Adams has tried to keep the conversation open. He has avoided criticism of Parr.

'I think things are going very well,' replied Parr. 'I've been pretty busy as you know on this new planning project, but I've got the job done on time.'

'Good,' said Adams. 'I read the report. I think it's excellent. Who helped you with the job?'

'I did it by myself,' replied Parr, proudly. 'It meant me working over a few nights last week and spending most of the weekend on it, but I eventually did it.'

'You mean no one helped?' inquired Adams.

'I didn't need anyone. Besides, I got the job done more quickly doing it all by myself,' Parr replied.

'Well this is the sort of thing that I have been talking about,' said Adams, getting angry. 'I've been doing your supervising job while you have been doing this project. Twice last week people from your section came to me and asked for my help on their work, because they said you had told them not to bother you as you were busy. On another occasion, one of your men came and said he was not going to be able to finish a job on time, and could he have some assistance. At that time, there were three men in your section who were free and available to help out both you and the other man. Don't you think you should have been looking at the organization of the work in your section?'

'Well, they are all fairly experienced men in the section. I don't need to chase them. They always manage to get things sorted out. Besides, I was busy doing this planning project for you.'

'The planning project is only one job. As the section manager you have the task of organizing all the work of the group.'

'We get our work done.'

'Yes, but at a cost. As I see it, you keep all the interesting jobs. Below you, some men are overworked and others have little to do. As you reserve the new work for yourself, no one learns much except you. The rest of your men are getting bored doing routine work.'

'I get paid more than they do because I can deal with these difficult jobs.'

The conversation has now begun to take an argumentative turn. Adams has clearly indicated he disapproves of Parr's mode of working, but feels he is not making any impact. Parr defends his behaviour and feels he has done a sound technical job. Adams feels that he needs to change the conversation. He had originally set out to help Parr: he is still trying, but has now found himself to be not getting very far. Parr defends stoutly, feeling he is in the right.

'Look,' said Adams, 'I think we are getting into an argument. What I'm saying is that the technical side of your work is excellent. I want your managerial side to be as good. Now, how about going on a management-training course. It may be just the thing that will enable you to deal with some of these supervisory problems.'

Adams summarizes his view of the problem, and prescribes what he feels may be a solution. However, Parr does not share Adams's definition of the problem and is not keen on the solution.

'I've been in this sort of work for ten years now,' said Parr. 'I don't know everything, but I think I've got a lot of experience. I don't see that a management course would help me. I'll go if you say so, but I don't feel that my section will do any better than it is at present.'

'Well I feel there is need for some improvement. Maybe we should make Jack Graham in your section your assistant manager so as to get the administrative things sorted out,' said Adams.

'No, I don't think that would work,' replied Parr, defensively. 'Jack is a good bloke at his job but I don't want him or anyone else getting in my way.'

The Choice

Whatever Adams suggests is being blocked or diverted by Parr. For some reason, Adams is not succeeding. He is trying to help but the help is not accepted.

This conversation could happen in most organizations. The manager Adams, in this situation, becomes frustrated and angry. Why does the supervisor, Parr, refuse his help? The answer is not easy and may depend on a number of factors.

It may be that:

1. The supervisor does not accept the problem as defined by Adams, that he (Parr) fails to supervise.

2. He may acknowledge the problem, but refuse to admit it as his fault.

3. The superior puts over his help in a manner which the subordinate sees as a negative criticism rather than positive help.

4. The supervisor feels things are proceeding as he wishes and any help would only change the situation without accruing any benefit.

Clearly, Adams in the above situation is in a difficult position. He feels Parr is not doing the supervisory aspect of his work, whereas it should take up half his time. Instead, Parr devotes all his time to the technical aspect of the job and gets fully involved and over-committed on particular tasks. Adams does not wish to lose his best technical man, but he cannot have one section working inefficiently because the supervisor does not manage.

Adams feels at a loss. This is reinforced by the fact that he is likely to have to make some men redundant if the company's business does not improve. Eventually, Adams confronts Parr with the choice.

'Well we have discussed this a long time. It seems to me your skills lie on the technical not the managerial side of the job. How about moving in to another section at the same salary, with a senior-associate title, where you can concentrate on advanced technical jobs?' said Adams.

'I enjoy my present job. I feel I've got the opportunity both to do advanced work and supervise at the same time,' replied Parr. 'Being a senior associate would mean I would lose my managerial position.'

'Look, I'm only trying to help you.'

'Well it doesn't sound like that to me. It sounds as if you want to get rid of me.'

The gap between the two men is now quite wide. Adams's attempts to help are seen by Parr as an effort to undermine his position. Something has clearly gone wrong. Adams has made it clear he does not wish to lose Parr. Parr either has not heard him, or does not believe him.

Who Required Help?

This case provides a basis upon which to examine some of the problems associated with helping another person. Actually, Adams wanted to put the problem of Parr's inadequate supervision to him and offer help in dealing with the situation. The first difficulty emerged when Parr said he felt that things were going well. To him, there was no problem. Indeed, Adams had to agree that the project planning report he had just received from Parr was excellent. However, the conversation from there took a distinct turn, and the two men began to move away from each other.

Adams, upon finding that Parr had done the job all by himself, became critical of Parr's use of his time. The strategy used by Adams was to point out, in what he thought was a logical way, all the problems that arose. Parr perceived this as an attack rather than a problem-solving discussion. He, therefore, sought to justify his action by saying he was paid to do technical work.

Was Adams's strategy appropriate? Rather than outlining his views and making judgements, he could have adopted a different approach. He could have asked Parr for help. There was no guarantee it would have resolved the problem, but it was less likely to create the conflict than Adams's original approach. He could, for example, have said: 'Well, Bob, I need your help to sort some things out. You see last week, while you were engaged on that project, some of your men came and asked me to sort out the allocation of work. I feel that I shouldn't be interfering in such matters. How do you feel about this part of the job?'

Here, Adams provides Parr with information without trying to be critical. He indicates he has a personal problem which by inference is related to Parr and the way he organizes his job. He ends by asking an open-ended question about Parr's feelings on the issue. If, at this point, Parr had said he did not feel it was his job, then clearly action would need to be taken to establish what the job included. If he said that the men could look after themselves, Adams could say this created problems for him in which he wanted Parr's help. At this point, Parr has a choice whether to help or say that he feels, for whatever reason, that it is not possible for him to change his existing approach.

PROBLEM-SOLVING STRATEGIES: AN ANALYSIS

Adams realized the approach he had taken was leading into a win/lose conflict situation and tried to change the direction of the discussion. He prescribed, firstly, a training course which was turned down. Second, he prescribed the appointment of an assistant manager. Again, this was rejected. The solutions Adams develops at this stage leave the decision to Parr. However, Parr feels that the solutions are irrelevant as they do not relate to what he regards as a problem.

At the next stage of the meeting, Adams takes on a negotiative relationship. He puts forward a bargain that Parr can do technical work at the same salary in another section providing he gives up his managerial post. This Parr does not agree with. Adams is now in a dilemma. Does he continue to bargain? Should he make a decision and issue Parr with a directive? Should he reconsider again what the problem is and adopt a consultative and reflective approach? What should his strategy be?

HELPING APPROACHES

Adams decided to think before he acted. In doing this, he went to a number of people and told them of the situation.

He put the problem in the following way to these people. 'The man in question has been a supervisor of a section for over a year. During this time, he has turned out excellent technical reports, but has totally failed to manage the work of people in his section. I am in a moral dilemma. If I move him to a new section he will lose his managerial position and will be on the list for redundancy, should any more people be required to leave. If he stays in his present job as a manager, there is little danger of him being made 'redundant, but the work of the section will get worse. I can't allow that to happen as people there may be made redundant and questions will be asked about my control over the area. I seem to be caught between two equally unattractive alternatives.'

1. *Consultative Control*

The first man he talked to, John Armfield, asked him a series of questions. How old was Parr? How many children did he have? What sort of a person was he? What salary was he on? Had his job been written down? Did Parr see Adams as a threat? What were Parr's feelings about his men? These and many more questions were asked, but Adams was not sure what it was all leading to. The man seemed genuinely interested and wanting to help, but all he did was ask questions, some of which Adams could not answer and others he thought irrelevant.

Here was a person trying to help Adams, but again not getting far. Armfield's strategy was to gather as much information as possible. Once he had sufficient information, he would feel in a position to suggest (prescribe) some answers. He, therefore, adopted a consultative approach but controlled the area for discussion. The focus of the discussion was not on what Adams wanted to say, but on the information Armfield felt he required. Adams, therefore, found himself responding to issues raised by the questioner who thereby controlled the conversation. Moreover, no particular point was developed. The questioner hedge-hopped from inquiries about Parr's salary, to his family, his views about Adams, his personality, and so on. Moreover, Armfield centred his questions mainly on Parr, rather than Adams.

Adams eventually decided to close the conversation. He thanked the man for his help, but felt he had received very little. Adams felt he had talked a lot, but the other man had not really understood his problem.

2. *Prescriptive Judgement*

The next person he talked to, Roy Dale, was sharp and to the point. 'Look,' he said, 'why don't you set this bloke up in a department of his own. Either that or give him the push. I can't see why you are so worried about one man.' With this quick solution-centred response he offered a prescription and dismissed the problem as one of not much importance. Adams was not looking for an easy prescription. While he valued the suggestion, he felt the problem needed more thought.

3. *Negotiative Exchange*

Bill Patterson, a manager at a similar level in one of the operating companies of the organization, took a different approach. To Adams's surprise, his colleague became very solution-centred and proposed a swap. The other manager had in his department a man with sound potential as a manager, but only average technical ability. There was, however, no opportunity for his man to move upwards in the company. 'I'm looking for a good technical man. Why don't we arrange an exchange?' Adams thought through the idea and decided to postpone a decision. He already had a successor in mind from within his own team. Patterson's idea was useful, although it didn't really deal with the problem as Adams saw it.

4.   Directive Instructions

Adams considered asking Frank Tasker, his own boss, what to do. He knew what Tasker's response would be. He would help in his own way by providing a quick-fire solution which would have the effect of a command. Tasker was renowned for his directive approach. Adams also knew Tasker was intolerant of incompetence and would most likely direct that Parr should be made redundant.

5.   Reflective Understanding

Finally, Adams met Phil Robins who was in the training department. Robins listened to the problem. 'You feel this is a moral dilemma?' he said, reflecting back Adams's concern. 'That to me is the heart of the matter,' said Adams. 'The man in question is not incompetent. He's one of the best engineering project planners that this company has or will have. But, to my mind, he's in the wrong job and he can't see it.'

'You feel he would be better employed elsewhere?' summarized Robins. 'Yes, but I don't feel that we should sack him. Not just because he's got a wife and a few kids. Most of us have families to look after. Parr is a real asset, and I'm concerned that we don't lose his talent.'

'You are concerned that the company might lose this man?' reflected Robins, in a manner that invited Adams to continue. 'Yes,' said Adams, 'even if I move him to a new section he would be demoted and might leave. On the other hand, if redundancies occur then being last into a new section he would have to be first out. Either way, we might lose him.'

The conversation continued. Robins offered no advice or solutions, but just encouraged Adams to talk without seeking to judge his comments. After half an hour, Robins said to Adams, 'Where do you feel you are on this problem now?'

'Well,' said Adams, 'I've had a good think about the alternatives open to me. It seems I can go and discuss with Parr one more time how his work could be reorganized. Alternatively, I could demote him at the same pay into another section, transfer him, or make him redundant. Is that how you see it?'

This was the first question Adams had put directly to Robins. Clearly, Adams was interested in hearing any alternatives Robins may have. 'I see it very much as you have outlined, but is it possible that you could use this man's technical ability in a special role where he reports to you direct without having subordinates,' said Robins.

'That's another interesting possibility,' said Adams. 'I hadn't considered that. Now let's consider how I can discuss these ideas with Parr.' 'What do you want to achieve in this meeting?' asked Robins. 'I need to start right, this time. Maybe, I could learn from the last effort,' Adams said. 'In what way?' inquired Robins.

'Well I need to be less critical and give Parr more room in which to think and talk. Last time, I stressed I was trying to help him, but he didn't feel that way. This time, I must avoid trying to sell him my solution and give him an opportunity to consider the alternatives as I have done.'

'How do you feel that is best done?'

'I'm not sure, but I think I have got to get over my problem without giving Parr a guilt complex. I think I will have to be straightforward with Parr and tell him that, while his job as section manager must come to an end, between us we should try and work out a scheme that enables him to stay with the company and do the job for which he is best fitted.'

Adams thanked Robins for his help and went away feeling that he now was clearer in his mind what needed to be done.

AN ASSESSMENT OF INTERPERSONAL HELP

Here is a case where the nature of help is not easy to define. The problem is a complex one. The implications of the decision taken affect the livelihoods of numerous people. Such decisions cannot be taken lightly, but the criteria for making such decisions are not always clear.

1. Closed-Ended Problems

Sometimes, the criteria for decisions and for help are well established. If, for example, someone asks you to direct him to a railway station, then he will welcome being told in a directive or prescriptive solution-centred manner the quickest route. He will not normally welcome such reflective questions as 'You feel you want to know where the railway station is?' Such a response would be irrelevant. The person in question has diagnosed his problem clearly and now wants a solution.

Thus, with certain problems, which we shall call *closed-ended problems*, the provision of information, material, or action to resolve the issue is required of the helper. This applies wherever a person has clearly defined the problem and is asking for a solution. It applies in such situations as when a car engine breaks down and you request a mechanic to mend it. You don't expect him to inquire after your reasons, only to get the car going again.

2. Open-Ended Problems

However, where the problem is not clearly stated or understood, it is important for the helper to become problem-centred. He may need to ask consultative questions or be reflective. Where strong feelings and emotion are displayed by the presenter of the problem, it is usually better for the helper to act as a mirror to reflect back the concerns of the presenter. This enables the presenter to talk through his problem and thereby clarify in his mind the issues at stake. The skill of the helper here is to reflect in an understanding way the central issues without seeking to judge or pass comment on the presenter's ideas. Identifying the critical issues and learning to avoid evaluation or attributing things to the other person, are difficult skills to grasp. This can be a very powerful form of help.

When we are asked to help, there is in most of us a feeling that we should offer a solution. After all, why did the person ask for help? However, it is important to distinguish when it is appropriate to offer a solution or just help clarify the problem. If a person like Bob Parr came to you as a friend and said 'I'm not sure whether I should leave my job. What do you think I should do?' what response would be appropriate? Does he really want you to say 'Yes, Bob, I think you ought to leave' or 'No, I would suggest you stick it out?' In such a situation, your opinion is not likely to be of much relevance as you do not know the situation fully, nor Bob's feelings, and, most important of all, you do not have to live with the consequences of the decision. In such a situation, it would be more appropriate to enable Parr to talk about the problem.

THE CONTROL OF THE PROCEEDINGS

A central issue that needs to be faced in helping people with interpersonal problems concerns who is going to control the problem-solving process. If you have a high degree of knowledge that will solve the problem and your solution is likely to be acceptable, you can afford to control the discussion and be solution-centred. However, where either knowledge or the acceptability of solutions is low, the discussion needs to be controlled by the person presenting the problem. The role of the helper in such situations is to facilitate the development of the presenter's problem-solving activity.

There is a tendency often to try to take a problem from a person and hand him back a prepacked solution which he is left to implement without understanding how the solution was arrived at, or what it involves.

Whose Problem?

The important question to ask is: Whose problem is it? If a person says to a dentist, 'My tooth hurts and I want it dealt with', this is an indication that the patient is willing for the dentist to take over accountability for resolving the problem. There are, however, many problems which cannot be transferred: they must remain the property of the presenter. To try to take over some problems means taking over a person's job or indeed trying to live his life for him. When, for example, a person says he's not sure what job he should have, it is impossible to take such a problem from him. It is, however, possible to help him think through his solution, but that is all.

Ultimately, help is determined by the recipient. It is therefore to the recipient, the presenter of the problem, that attention needs to be directed. What is he saying? What is he seeking? Where does he wish the conversation to go? The helper then has to decide if he wishes to go along with, or has the capability to go along with, the presenter. If the answer is yes, the difficulty is staying with the presenter without getting blinded by the problem.

Conclusion

In managerial problem solving, the danger is that people try to take over other's problems and foist their solutions upon the presenter of the problem. Managers feel under pressure to do this daily because time is short. The result is that we offer help, but without success. Sometimes we are behaving in a non-helpful way because we have not listened carefully to what the presenter of the problem wishes us to do. Thus, at times, we are problem-centred in our approach when we should be solution-centred. At other times, we are solution-centred when we should be problem-centred. The results speak for themselves, but usually this is too late. We need to be able to detect the appropriate behaviour to use at a given time. This can be done if we recognize the alternative interpersonal problem-solving approaches and recognize the behavioural cues being offered by others.

Summary

A. In this chapter, attention has been drawn to behavioural aspects of giving and receiving help, in which consideration of the following issues has taken place:
  - The nature of help.
  - The need for help.
  - Various approaches to help.
  - An assessment of help in problem solving.
B. In particular, the chapter should enable the manager to:
  - Assess the problems of offering help.
  - Identify alternative approaches.
  - Recognize the situation for problem-centred and solution-centred behaviour.
  - Understand who should control the conversation.
C. In considering the issues raised, the manager should ask himself:
  - How often do I have to give help in problem identification and solution generation?
  - How do people react when I am trying to be helpful?
  - Who controls the discussions I have with subordinates, colleagues, superiors when help is required?
  - What must I do to develop my skills in interpersonal help further?

14

GETTING CORNERED: A DANGER IN MANAGERIAL PROBLEM SOLVING

PROPOSITION AND OPPOSITION

Getting cornered in managerial situations is easy. Getting out of corners is difficult. To be cornered is to have one or more other people exposing and trying to undermine your ideas as you try to defend them.

A typical example occurred on a training course. The managing director, a man called Pearson, came along to introduce a new course for senior managers on appraisal interviewing. He took some time outlining the system whereby to ensure the development of the best men in the organization. Records were to be kept of men's progress, and annual interviews conducted. These interviews were designed to be 'informal' and allow the subordinates to talk over any career problems.

When the superior had finished, he asked if there were any questions. The first few questions were polite and non-threatening, in which people asked for more information about procedural matters. Then one man said, 'I'm not sure whether this appraisal-system idea can work. Talking with a man once a year, and filling in forms, does not to my mind tackle the real problems.'

Pearson had to choose at this point. He could open up the conversation by reflecting back to the man, 'You feel that there are big problems in this area?' Or he could close the conversation down to a win/lose approach. He chose the latter and an argument, rather than a discussion, began.

The way Pearson got cornered was to fight back on the points he had already made. 'I realize the problems,' he said, 'but they must be overcome.

No system is perfect but it is up to us to make it work. Now, I and many others have spent long hours developing this new system. Our aim is to try to get a reasonably objective assessment of a man's ability.'

'With respect, Sir,' started another subordinate, with the clear indication that he did not respect his boss's opinion, 'I don't see how it is possible to get an objective assessment of people when they are being assessed by different people.'

'Well that is why we have designed the assessment form, where you are asked to judge a man on such things as loyalty, punctuality, creativity, leadership, and so on within a scale of five points,' replied the boss.

At this stage, Pearson is well and truly cornered. Each time he makes a point, his subordinates counter it with another.

Point Counter Point

'I see that,' replied another subordinate, 'but where one man gives a score of four, I might give three, and vice versa.'

'Well we have been very careful in our wording of the points on the scale to try and prevent such confusion. I'm sure if you read the document clearly you will see this.'

The last sentence is the sort of comment a person makes when he realizes he is being pinned down on the defensive, and feels he must attack in order to get out and win. The trouble is, however, that this usually has the opposite effect. The opposition are annoyed at the attack and press more strongly. They feel they have a good logical case which is not being heard, and resent being upbraided for not complying with a system they oppose.

'Yes, I have read the wording a number of times, but I found it ambiguous. I'm sure whoever worded it did his best, but it is just not good enough. I think he is fooling himself if he believes it solves the problem. I'm not sure whether we can have such a thing as a system to appraise people.'

So the argument continued. On one side, is Pearson, putting forward a proposition he wants others to accept. On the other side, are the subordinates, who are not committed to the idea, and are indicating that it is not acceptable. What really concerns them in such situations is that the boss does not seem to listen to their views. He has closed the conversation down to views for or against his proposals. In effect, the following situation is operating:

BOSS	SUBORDINATES
1	1
My proposal	*Your proposal is*
is good because	*inadequate because* ....

This is not really a dialogue in the full meaning of the term. One person tries to defend a proposition, others seek to attack it. Energy is wasted on both sides. It is a common enough occurrence.

A PROBLEM-CENTRED ALTERNATIVE

Pearson did have an alternative. As soon as it was indicated that there might be difficulties, he could have opened up the meeting into a problem-centred discussion. As indicated earlier, he could have done this by just saying 'You feel there are problems in this area?' and then listened. It is likely that a more creative discussion, rather than an argument, would have taken place. Let us, for example, consider how it might have proceeded.

'Yes, I feel there are problems,' says a subordinate. 'I'm not sure appraisal interviews can do any more than we accomplish on a day to day basis.'

'You feel you have enough time to discuss with the men their career progress on a day to day basis?' Pearson might reflect.

'Not all the time, but we do know what our subordinates are thinking.'

'You feel that you know their views?' Pearson might say.

'Yes, to a large extent. There may be points from time to time when this is not so with some individuals.'

'You feel it might be useful to see these people from time to time?'

'I think it could be helpful.'

'Then perhaps the appraisal system needs to be more flexible. How do you feel for example about the appraisal interview as a means for giving a man information on how he is doing in the job?'

'I think this can be quite useful,' another subordinate might reply, 'but I disagree with these rating scales you have given us on loyalty, creativity, leadership, and so on.'

'You feel these are not helpful?'

'Well it's hard to make such a judgement. What I regard as a "three" another person may call "four". I agree that some uniformity is necessary, but I doubt if this is the way to do it.'

'You feel improvements could be made?' Pearson might say, still keeping the discussion going.

'I think we ought to rely more on what a man has done during the year. I think his performance on given jobs should be written down and comments made upon it rather than vague scores on things like creativity. Furthermore, I think the subordinate should be allowed to write down each year what he feels he has achieved. After all, this is of vital importance.'

'Those are valuable ideas which I have written down. Obviously, we need to examine this issue again in the light of these comments.'

Here, is a much more open and positive debate where new ideas emerge rather than a circular argument.

The Change of Meeting

The conversation has led to the exchange of people's feelings about the proposal and new ideas have been developed. Pearson showed concern for the views of the subordinates, rather than trying to sell his own ideas regardless of what they said. The importance of conducting a discussion rather than an argument is that energy tends to be directed to diagnosing the problems as well as evaluating solutions.

In the first presentation, when Pearson put forward his solution to the problem he had diagnosed, his solution was not seen by his subordinates to be as relevant to the problem. In such cases, it is imperative that he should revert to a problem-centred approach and try to gather more information. In the first presentation, he used a combination of directive and prescriptive approaches, and the meeting was dominated by people who were trying to score points by logical argument. In the second, he adopted a more reflective and consultative behaviour. In effect, he changed the nature of the meeting from a *command* approach to an *advisory* one, and the meeting emphasized people's feelings rather than the accumulation of logical points.

INTERROGATION

Cornering can be played many ways. Often, it is used in the form of an interrogation. This is useful if you are trying to pin someone down, for example, gaining an admission of guilt from a criminal, but not necessarily so when discussing employee work performance.

In another interview, a manager, let us call him Mr Roper, was conducting a performance review with one of his subordinates, John Simpson. Roper was concerned by Simpson's over-strictness in his dealing with his own subordinates. He had, for example, told off one of the secretaries in public for having an untidy desk, and on another occasion upbraided a young clerk publicly for producing 'sloppy figures which no one can read'. The girl had gone home crying, and the young clerk handed in his resignation the following week.

Roper felt he had to discuss these matters with Simpson and make sure that the latter improved his relationships in the office. Roper was unsure how to start. After an initial chat about the weekend and the family, the boss asked: 'How is the job going?'

'I've no complaints,' said Simpson, 'things are going quite well.'

'Good,' replied Roper, 'I'm pleased things are going as planned. I was sorry to see young Marsden resign last week, though. I thought he had the makings of a solid performer. He gave as his reason for leaving that you "were always getting at him".'

'Well he would say that', said Simpson. 'As far as I was concerned, I just did my job and asked him to do his properly. He was far too slack in his presentation of material. Admittedly, he got it right, but it took him ages and it was almost impossible to read his reports.'

'Yes, but would you agree with me that there are right and wrong ways of going about correcting a person's mistakes?' asked Roper.

Clearly, here is an implied criticism, and Roper is cornering Simpson who cannot really disagree with the question, even if he wanted to.

'Yes I agree with you, but young Marsden needed a telling off. It wasn't the first time he had produced poor quality work,' replied Simpson defensively.

'Well, don't you feel that telling him off in the office was the wrong place?' inquired Roper, implying that it was, and further cornering Simpson.

'No, I think a public example had to be made and I deliberately let him know my views in front of the others,' replied Simpson, trying to fight his way out of the corner.

Roper felt Simpson fighting back and responded: 'Would you agree with me that it could have been done another way to get the same result, without having Marsden leave us? After all, we have spent three years training him to do that job.'

'I don't know,' replied Simpson, sensing that Roper was bent on winning his point. 'I thought I was doing the right thing.'

'Well, discipline is a good thing, but I feel you have been a bit too heavy this time,' replied Roper, driving home his advantage. 'Try and be a bit more diplomatic next time.'

The Effect of Cornering

Here, Simpson has been reprimanded in a manner similar in its effect to that which he used on Marsden. Simpson has been put in a corner and is not allowed to escape until he concedes the point or admits defeat. Roper has himself made the same mistake as Simpson. The real issue, however, is what effect such behaviour has. Does it motivate people to greater efforts, and improvements, or does it make them resentful, inclined to withdraw, and work less effectively?

In the above case, the strategy of Roper was to pin Simpson down, by closing the conversation on specific issues. Throughout, Roper implied that Simpson was in the wrong and could thus be seen to have sided with the subordinate Marsden. Roper left little room for discussion. Simpson was asked either to agree or disagree with his boss. In most situations, this means the subordinate has to say, in effect, 'How right you are, Sir, and how wrong I was', or try to stand up against the man who probably controls his wages, his promotion chances, and his future employment with the company. Usually, the subordinate will grudgingly accept the boss's views while in the interview, then release his real feelings either on his subordinates or his family.

The subordinate is not likely to be highly motivated to improve his performance. First, his management methods have been criticized, second, he has received little help in how to improve them. Third, he has been cornered with little opportunity offered for a joint discussion of the problem.

THE DIAGNOSTIC APPROACH

If the meeting had been a managerial problem solving one, then it could have developed in the following way. Here the emphasis moves to problem diagnosis, rather than criticism and forced solutions.

ROPER: How is the job going?

SIMPSON: I've no complaints. Things are going quite well.

ROPER: You feel that things are going smoothly?

SIMPSON: Well, we have day to day problems like everyone else, but there is nothing which we can't handle. We are a bit short staffed at the moment as Marsden has left, and one of the secretaries is off.

ROPER: Well, if you need some extra help there, let me know. I noticed that Marsden had handed in his resignation. What happened?

SIMPSON: Well, it could be a lot of things, but I think he wasn't up to standard and he knew it.

ROPER: You feel he wasn't good enough?

SIMPSON: Yes, he took twice as long as I would expect to do a job and then handed in a shoddy report. He came up with the right answers, but that in itself was not good enough.

ROPER: You expected more from him?

SIMPSON: Well, he had been with us for three years and had a good training. His attitude to the job was sloppy. I had to have a word with him about it.

ROPER: How did he take it?

SIMPSON: He said nothing. It was like talking to a brick wall. But it served as an example to the others.

ROPER: You feel that was the best approach?

SIMPSON: Well, he needed telling. Perhaps I acted a little impulsively, but it's done now.

ROPER: You felt you acted a bit hastily?

SIMPSON: On reflection, maybe I did. Perhaps I should have spoken to him privately. I've snapped at one or two people recently without thinking. I probably upset one of the secretarial girls the other day when I was under pressure for some work to be done.

ROPER: You feel this happens when under pressure?

SIMPSON: Yes, usually. Take the girl I mentioned. She produced some letters and had put all the wrong addresses on them. They were urgent and I just exploded, I suppose I should try and control my anger. It's just that I'm keen to make sure the job goes well.

ROPER: You don't like mistakes?

SIMPSON: I believe I should set high standards for others to follow. However, I seem to lack skills in communicating with people.

ROPER: You feel this is an area where you could improve?

SIMPSON: Yes, maybe I need some training in these new methods. What would you suggest?

ROPER: That could be a sound idea for your future career development. Maybe we can invite the training manager over and see what he suggests. I think your idea is a positive way of making sure that the human aspects of management in your section are improved.

Here Roper has not tried to criticize, but rather encourage Simpson to talk about his work situation and problems. He has focused on developing a problem-solving discussion, rather than trying to corner and score points off Simpson. As the interview progressed, Simpson became more and more open, even diagnosing his own problem and suggesting his own solution. Roper acted as a mirror against which Simpson could talk out his problem and see himself more clearly.

This method is the opposite of a win/lose argument. It emphasizes getting the man with the problem to talk about it and become open to the point of self-criticism. Further, Roper avoids making solution suggestions until Simpson asks for help on a particular issue. At this stage, Roper proffers a possible solution.

This example is designed especially to illustrate a different approach from that we have termed 'cornering'. In reality, an interview may never go as smoothly as this. The point, however, relates to whether the more open problem-centred approach is worth trying. This can only be answered in terms of the objectives that the interviewer has. If his aim is to get his subordinate to think about his behaviour, to adopt a self-critical, self-reforming style, then this approach may work. If, however, the superior feels he should punish, criticize, reprimand, and reform his subordinate, then maybe the first presentation is more appropriate.

Conclusion

This chapter has tried to illustrate two different approaches in dealing with meetings. The common theme has been that of the dangers involved in getting cornered. It identifies some of the behaviour associated with such a situation, and suggests possible methods to get out of it.

You can get cornered particularly when:

1. You are presenting a proposal for acceptance by others, which they have reservations about and seek to bring to your attention. If you reinforce your proposition without regard to the points being made against it, others may seek to corner you and dismantle your ideas one by one on a logical point by point basis.

2. You are appraising someone's performance, whom you feel could have behaved in a different manner on certain issues. If you attack and criticize the individual, he is likely to defend his behaviour. He will close up or maybe withdraw or possibly launch a counter-attack. Sometimes, he will just repeat his explanations *ad nauseam*. If he does these things, then he will feel cornered and his behaviour will be designed as a means of escape. The

alternative is to have a problem-solving discussion during which the other person is encouraged to talk about his problems and to develop his own ideas for improvements. He may also request your ideas and listen to them.

It is easy to get into corners, difficult to get out of them. This chapter identifies some of the behaviour associated with cornering and points to approaches that can be used to overcome this problem.

Summary

A. In this chapter, attention has been drawn to the problems of being cornered in managerial problem solving, involving:
   - The nature of proposals.
   - The reaction of others.
   - The approach to dealing with resistance.
   - The importance of recognizing the problems others feel they have.

B. In particular, the chapter should enable the manager to:
   - Identify when he is getting into a 'corner' during managerial problem solving.
   - Distinguish the various approaches to coping with a cornered situation.
   - Assess the importance of exploring the other person's reactions.
   - Weigh the alternative strategies for avoiding 'corners'.

C. In considering the issues raised, a manager should ask himself:
   - How often do I find myself cornered?
   - What do I do in such situations?
   - Why do people try to corner me?
   - What is the result following a cornering incident?
   - What do I need to do on future occasions when I am cornered?

15

CONVERSATIONAL SEDUCTION

HOW THE CONVERSATION MOVES

'I'm lost,' said John Hardy, a sales representative with a retailing company. 'I don't know where we are or where we are going.' At the time he made these statements, Hardy was sitting firmly in a comfortable chair in the office of his sales manager in the centre of London. He was not lost in the geographical sense. His problem was that he was no longer able to discern the thread of the discussion that was taking place among the sales team of which he was a member.

'It seems to me that we are beginning to wander from one problem to another without dealing with any one in depth. If we don't stick to the point at hand we will talk all day and accomplish nothing,' concluded Hardy.

This chapter examines what happens during many group problem-solving meetings. People spend a lot of time talking, but wander from one point to another. Time and energy are wasted. Those in the meeting feel increasingly dissatisfied and start to get annoyed with one another. Our aim here, therefore, is to identify a central cause of inefficient group problem solving. This we shall call *conversational*, or *verbal*, *seduction*.

As an example, we shall consider the problem of Phil Blake who, as sales manager of Retail Fabrics, calls a meeting of his sales representatives. An organization chart is provided in Fig. 15.1, outlining those involved in the meeting.

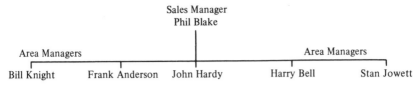

Fig. 15.1

THE CONTROL OF CONVERSATION

Blake wanted to examine how sales could be improved during the next six months. In particular, Blake wanted to show his men the new brochures which had been produced. His aim was to get the men motivated to sell the new clothing styles. After Blake had given his talk on the new brochure, he suggested that the group discuss any problems related to sales.

One of the representatives, Bill Knight, said he liked the new designs, but was concerned that he would have to spend a lot of time explaining the changes in the nature of the product to his clients. This would take up not only his time, but also the clients'. 'I have difficulty already getting the client to spend fifteen minutes with me while I get an order. This brochure means I'll have to spend at least thirty minutes with every client, explaining the changes in price and design. This means I'll only be able to do half my normal calls.'

'You can leave the brochure with them and let them go through it,' said Blake. 'They can always ask questions, if they don't understand it.'

'Well, it's taken you nearly half an hour to explain the changes to us,' replied Knight. 'Besides, my clients may have so many brochures given them they put most of them in the refuse bin,' retorted Knight. 'As I see it we are going to have difficulty keeping up our existing sales, particularly if delivery dates are not met.'

'I'm worried about delivery,' said Frank Anderson. 'The last time we introduced new designs the production people got in a hell of a mess. There were delays of up to three weeks on delivery.'

'The production side say that things are running according to schedule and there should be no problem,' replied the sales manager.

'That's what they said last time,' replied Anderson. 'I lost three customers over that farce. I hope it's not going to happen all over again.'

'They have got this new manager in charge of production,' replied the manager. 'He has reorganized the system by use of organization and methods study techniques. He's also introduced a lot of new machinery.'

'It's about time they got sorted out,' replied Anderson. 'The last time I was down there it looked like something out of the nineteenth century.'

It was at this point, that John Hardy interjected to say he was lost and did not know what was happening. 'Look,' said Hardy, 'two minutes ago we were discussing Bill's problem of how we get our clients to understand our new product range. Now we are discussing how well or badly the production department have or have not done their job. We are beginning to ramble.'

Hardy does not state what the group should discuss, but expresses his discontent with the way the conversation is beginning to jump from one topic to another. His intervention gave Blake a chance to guide the discussion into a different channel, or to criticize Hardy.

As it was, Frank Anderson took up the conversation again. 'You may be lost and think we are rambling, but when you've been in this job as long as me you'll know what I'm talking about. Unless those production people are organized, we might as well sit here and play cards.' Anderson, clearly, felt under attack from Hardy.

'We should be thinking about our job and how we can improve, rather than moaning about the past.' Here, Hardy used another emotive word, 'moaning', which follows upon his 'rambling.'

Anderson clearly was becoming annoyed. 'No one is moaning yet,' he replied bitterly. 'I'm just saying we've got to make sure that the production side do their job. If things go wrong, I'll bet you are one of the first to shout.'

Blake has had an opportunity to restructure the conversation, but missed it. As a result, the discourse moves onto another level with Anderson and Hardy entering into a verbal battle. Blake and the group are being verbally seduced.

THE NATURE OF CONVERSATIONAL SEDUCTION

Conversational seduction occurs regularly. It involves one or more members of a group subtly changing the direction of the discussion from one topic to another so that the original topic is not dealt with, but neither is it totally rejected. When Hardy made his initial intervention, he was raising the question as to whether the group had moved from the stated task of discussing how to improve sales during the next six months. He felt that the seduction process had already begun. To him, the group was moving away from its central task.

However, Hardy himself also began to be seduced. Having raised his question, he was attacked by Anderson who took an objection to Hardy's implied criticism of him. By responding to this attack and using a further emotive expression, Hardy encouraged the seduction process which he originally was trying to stop. As the argument between the two men continues the discussion moves even further away from how to improve sales in the next six months. Hardy has become a victim of the seduction process. He could have stopped the process by saying he was lost and not sure where the conversation was leading. This leaves it to others to make judgements. His second error was to respond to Anderson, and to use an emotional approach. In doing so, he got locked into a conversation which he had initially felt was irrelevant, and the group wandered further from the original point.

The model in Fig. 15.2 identifies one way of thinking about these problems.

Time

		PAST	PRESENT	FUTURE
	Me	(1) My personal development and experience	(2) My current feelings, situation, and problems	(3) My future expectations, plans, and investments
	You	(4) Your personal development and experience	(5) Your current feelings, situation, and problems	(6) Your future expectations, plans, and investments
Subjects	Us	(7) Our personal development and experience	(8) Our current feelings, situation, and problems	(9) Our future expectations, plans, and investments
	Them	(10) Their personal development and experience	(11) Their current feelings, situation, and problems	(12) Their future expectations, plans, and investments
	Things	(13) Their development, use, and value	(14) Their current state, position, and value	(15) Their future use and value

Fig. 15.2 Communication levels

Areas for Conversational Focus

The above matrix examines possible relationships of given subjects and time periods in a discussion. In all, according to this simplified model, there are fifteen possible areas upon which to focus discussion. There is no reason to assume that in any discussion one should confine oneself to one area, or range over all. However, it is useful to know the major areas one is trying to concentrate on.

For example, in this case, Phil Blake said the aim of the meeting was to look at how sales could be improved within six months. The initial focus therefore, according to Blake, who by his statement is trying to control the focus of conversation, is on the future. However, Blake brings into the discussion a brochure (a *thing* in our model) which relates to the present. Therefore, the total initial focus is on *us*, the sales group, in terms of the *present* problem of the new brochure (*things*), together with a concern for our (*us*) sales (*things*) over the next six months (*future*). The boundaries for conversation set by Blake's initial statement, therefore, cover areas 8, 14, 9, and 15. Clearly, there is in Blake's request for a discussion of the issues a recognition of the need to enter into the personal areas 2, 3, 5, and 9.

However, as the discussion proceeds it moves into an examination of what the production department (*them*) had done when the last change had been made (*past*) and centred on area 10. Anderson later wanted to move to his personal (*me*) experience (*past*) of dealings with the production (*them*) people over such matters. This moved the conversation into areas 1 and 10. As Hardy became involved in the argument, the focus moved to areas 1 and 4.

In such a situation, Blake, the manager, needs to ask himself whether or not he and others in the group are being seduced away from the topic he established in the initial stage. The question that has to be resolved is who determines the area upon which conversation shall take place. Clearly, in the example given, Blake lost control. Hardy tried to question the direction of the conversation and eventually ended up being seduced into an argument with Anderson, and thereby the group was led further away from its original task.

THE CONVERSATIONAL PARCEL

This example of seduction implies that the conversation between people should be at a certain point or level. The question is, who should decide this point. If a manager calls a meeting, as did Phil Blake, sets a clearly defined topic, and finds the discussion focusing on something else, then clearly someone else is beginning to control the discussion. The process by which this happens is called *verbal seduction.*

The point of raising this issue is that managers should be aware in a meeting of:

1. Where they want discussion to centre.
2. Where it is at various points in time.
3. When people seek to seduce them on to a different level of discussion.

It is important for managers to have a model for thinking about conversation (see Fig. 15.2). Then it is easier to ascertain when the discussion is moving away from the central topic of the agenda. All conversation can be thought of as a game of pass-the-parcel. However, during the discussion, the parcel changes shape and sometimes, as we have seen, people will try to introduce a new parcel. It is the manager's task not only to contribute to the group discussion, but monitor the passing of the conversational parcel.

Let us return to our original example of Phil Blake and his sales team and examine their discussion in terms of the passing-the-parcel example. Anderson had taken up Hardy's point about moaning and replied, 'If things go wrong, I'll bet you are one of the first to shout.' Hardy sat silently and Phil Blake took up the conversation :

BLAKE: All this is not getting us anywhere. Leave me to deal with the production people, I want us to discuss how we are going to improve sales in the next six months.

JOWETT: (*not having spoken so far in the discussion*) I think we have got to concentrate our efforts more in certain areas. At the moment, we are too spread out. Look at my area. I've 225 customers, all of whom are supposed to be visited once every two months. With all the travelling involved, it's not on.

ANDERSON: I agree. I think we should concentrate our sales activity on the cities and cut out a lot of this travelling to country villages.

HARRY BELL: (*entering the conversation*) I counted up last week and found I spent forty-five per cent of my time driving from one place to another.

BLAKE: We just can't cut down the sales area like that. That is a decision for the sales director. I will let him know what you think. However, why not let us have the organization and methods people in to look at how we organize our travel?

JOWETT: What do they know about sales? I've had dealings with these O & M people before at my last company. I'm against them trying to tell me how to do my job here.

BLAKE: I was not suggesting they tell us how to do our job, but they could look at how we organize our time.

JOWETT: I don't want anyone spying on me. The answer is simple. Cut out the visits to country towns and villages. It does not require an organization and methods man to tell us that.

BELL: Maybe we need more sales staff to cover the areas. Why not, for example, have some trainee-salesmen working in conjunction with each of us?

BLAKE: That would send costs up, and we are already over our budget for this year.

ANDERSON: Then I think we need a bigger budget. After all, without sales where would the company be?

JOWETT: I quite agree, the salesman is the life blood of the organization. If we are not bringing in the orders, then there is no work for anyone.

The conversation has continued, but has it progressed? Let us trace how the conversation has passed from one person to another:

A. Blake restates the ground for discussion – how to improve sales in six months.

B. Jowett proposes a solution in area 15 – change the sales areas (things).

C. Anderson agrees.

D. Bell supports with evidence.

E.   Blake parries the movement and suggests looking at us and who we are organized at present – area 2.

F.   Jowett rejects this, but does not mention that it was following an O & M study in his last job that he was made redundant – area 1.

G.   Blake defends his proposition – area 2.

H.   Bell puts forward his proposition – area 13, the employment of trainees (them).

I.   Blake provides a reason for rejecting this by referring to the present situation regarding the budget – area 14.

J.   Anderson moves to area 15 and proposes a larger budget, and then refers to the salesman's importance – areas 8 and 9.

K.   Jowett supports his views.

Managing the Conversational Process

The stage is set once again for the seduction process to begin. Unless someone redirects the conversation, a new parcel will have entered the ring labelled 'the importance of salesmen and a justification of their position'. This was originally not on the agenda, but could now be the central topic. Its contribution to solving the problem of how sales can be improved in six months is not immediately evident.

The sales group has prevented Blake so far from having the discussion centre on what they, the salesmen, do at present (areas 5 and 8), and what they will do in the future (areas 6 and 9). These are plainly felt to be delicate areas. The group, therefore, steers the conversation away from themselves to external things like trainee-salesmen, travelling budgets, organization and methods, and the importance of salesmen in the company.

Blake, for his part, is seen by the group to be against them and their solutions. When he produces a solution, the group feel it attacks them and their way of working. Blake is clearly in a difficult position. In essence, the group will not allow him to decide the areas within which the conversation shall take place. Whenever Blake tries to establish the areas, a member of the group takes up the conversational parcel and plants it in another area. In short, Blake wants to look at the sales group and the performance of its members here and now, and plan for the future. The group feels this may be 'too close for comfort' and keeps transferring the discussion to situations and people outside themselves.

The manager in this situation needs to consider carefully:

1. Why the group adopts this behaviour.

2. What he can do to present the areas he would like to have discussed in a way acceptable to the group.

A group may have various reasons for behaving in this way. In this case, they may legitimately feel that they cannot discuss how they as individuals and as a group can improve their work until other issues such as travel, budgets, and production-department behaviour, are dealt with. However, these issues can be regarded as a smoke screen that the group puts up to seduce the discussion away from that stated by the manager. In such an instance, it is likely the group feels anxious and under pressure. They may be concerned as to whether they can meet the level of sales expected, be worried about their income, or, indeed, their jobs and career.

A person faced with the situation that confronts the sales manager, Phil Blake, needs to become much more problem diagnostic in his approach. He needs to develop a problem-solving discussion where he spends time listening to the views of group members. He should not seek to judge or evaluate these views, but rather encourage their expression.

At present, Blake is not getting very far in his discussions. He makes a statement. This is followed by solution-orientated statements from his group such as calls to cut down travelling, increase the budget, provide more salesmen. Blake evaluates these and reacts negatively to these solutions. The group perceive that he is not a hundred per cent behind them. Blake puts his own solutions which the group in turn reject. Both sides are talking, but little progress is made. Propositions are followed by negative evaluation and rejection.

Facing up to Conversational Seduction

There are no easy answers in coping with the sort of problem which has been outlined above. However, one thing is clear. The manager needs to adopt a more problem diagnostic approach, in accordance with the managerial problem-solving model which has already been shown in chapter 2 and is repeated in Fig. 15.3.

MPS approach	Decision-maker	Orientation
Directive	Manager	Solution-centred
Prescriptive	Recipient	Solution-centred
Negotiative	Joint decision	Solution-centred
Consultative	Questioner	Problem-diagnostic
Reflective	Problem presenter	Problem-diagnostic

Fig. 15.3 Managerial problem-solving approaches

So far in the meeting, Blake has been trading prescriptions with his group. The members have put forward various suggestions as solutions. Blake has not really accepted these and put forward his own suggestions. He now has to consider becoming more reflective towards the views of his group.

Each member of the group has brought with him his own private agenda. These items concern an individual's anxieties, fears, prejudices, and suspicions. Knight is concerned about time spent with customers, Anderson about the production department, Bell about the time he spends driving and lack of staff, Jowett about the O & M department, Blake about sales in the next six months, and Hardy about the confusion in the meeting. Now, all these concerns may be valid. But they cannot all be dealt with simultaneously. The fact that the issues are raised, however, is important. They must not be ignored. It is incumbent upon the manager to organize the meeting so that each person feels his problem has been dealt with in a satisfactory manner. All issues must be dealt with on their merit. But one issue should not be used to seduce the meeting from other issues. Above all, the meeting must do more than send people away with good feelings. The discussion should form the basis for effective action.

In the above case, Blake ended up with more problems than when he began. He found the meeting started to go off course. The problems he faced were symptomatic of many which have been outlined in this book. Looking on from the outside, it is easier to see the issues confronting Blake. It is also tempting to suggest to him what sort of meeting he should have held, what sort of managerial problem-solving approaches were appropriate at given times, and how to have avoided verbal seduction.

However, as we all know from experience, it is much more difficult to see the issues clearly when you are in the hot-seat, chairing the meeting. Adopting the appropriate behaviour to help resolve group problems requires not only a knowledge of the various approaches, but practice in using them. This can be achieved through managerial development courses on behavioural and organizational skills, and above all else continual, daily practice of these skills in meetings.

Conclusion

This chapter has pointed out the problems facing a manager in running a meeting. It has shown that there is always a risk that the meeting will be seduced verbally from the issues that it was to discuss. It has also been shown that when this happens there is usually a point at which it is possible for the situation to be rescued. We then went on to examine the fact that in any one discussion there are several relevant areas which may be covered, and pointed out that it was essential for the manager to know exactly what these are if he is to control the meeting properly. We also saw that the manager must know how to make the areas he has chosen acceptable to the group.

Summary

A. In this chapter, attention has been drawn to the nature of conversational (verbal) seduction. This has involved an analysis of:
- How conversation moves from one issue to another.
- The control of conversation.
- The process of verbal seduction.
- The levels of communication.

B. In particular, the chapter should enable the manager to:
- Recognize the emergence of conversational seduction.
- Distinguish the various levels of conversation.
- Identify who is controlling the discussion.
- Assess the action he should take to cope with the seduction process.

C. In considering the issues raised, a manager should ask himself:
- How often are meetings which I attend seduced?
- What conversational parcels get thrown into the discussion?
- Do people get 'lost' in these meetings?
- How is the seduction process dealt with?
- Do I clearly establish the nature of meetings so everyone knows the boundaries and what is expected of them?
- What do I need to do to prevent my meetings being seduced?

16

MANAGING BUSINESS MEETINGS

PROBLEMS, SOLUTIONS, AND MEETINGS

A central theme of this book has been the importance of distinguishing problem diagnostic from solution-centred behaviour, but in many ways this text has been primarily problem diagnostic. It has identified issues in the area of managerial problem solving and has outlined factors that need to be tackled if business meetings are to be made more effective. The emphasis has been upon the presentation of concepts and a description of situations.

While this is a necessary task, it is more likely to tell the manager what to avoid, rather than what to do. Knowing what to avoid is important, but knowing what to do is vital. This postscript is therefore an attempt at defining some guidelines. This, of course, has been the most difficult part of writing the book. Diagnosing problems is not really a risky task, but prescribing solutions is. Implementing such solutions is even more difficult. I feel it incumbent upon me to make some solution-centred prescription on the issues we have considered. It is done with the caveat that these guidelines are not universally applicable. They are drawn up without specific knowledge of the varied situations that individual managers will face. They should therefore not be used as rules, but as prescriptions. That is, they should be tested on their merit and adopted only when appropriate. The decision, as in any solution-centred prescription, is yours and with it the risk of failure. There is also the possibility of success in an improved working relationship between colleagues and subordinates.

Trying out these ideas will not be easy for everyone. They will take some time to get used to. Moreover, your colleagues and subordinates may wonder what you are up to. Why are you changing the way meetings have previously been organized? They may be suspicious and try to go back to the old methods. The ideas put forward here are not a gimmick, or an easy technique. They are more a way of thinking; a way of doing; a way of managing.

Colleagues and subordinates will want to know why you do things the way you do. In this sense, managers who try to use these ideas will have also to introduce others to their way of operating if they are to avoid opposition. This will involve introducing others to the concepts outlined in the glossary at the end of the book. For those who try the ideas put forward here, there can only be one piece of prior advice: *be conscious of the need for problem-centred behaviour when putting forward a new solution.* The rest of this chapter outlines issues and guidelines on the conduct and management of business meetings.

THE CONDUCT OF BUSINESS MEETINGS
Agenda-Building
Time is frequently wasted in meetings because those attending do not have a common understanding of how to conduct the proceedings. The most common procedure which facilitates a common understanding is the setting of an agenda. Where an agenda is used, it is normal for issues that people wish to discuss to be identified prior to the meeting. Rarely is the procedure used of developing an agenda at the start of the meeting. Additional items that people wish to discuss are invariably brought up under 'any other business', when time is short.

Therefore, in any meeting, establish a basic understanding regarding procedures to be used. It is normally sound practice to ask all who have knowledge to contribute, and/or are involved in the acceptability of decisions to identify the subjects they wish to have on an agenda prior to a meeting.

However, at the beginning of the meeting it is equally necessary, but rarely done, to ask whether anyone wishes to add an item to the agenda. The value of this is that a member who comes to a meeting with a burning issue can make it known early, rather than get increasingly anxious that he will not get a hearing under the small amount of time left for 'any other business'. By identifying all issues at the beginning, it is also possible to decide priorities and allocate time appropriately. These two factors are central to the effective operation of any meeting.

In short, we can summarize the points relating to basic procedures as:

1. Allow members of the meeting to put forward agenda items prior to a meeting.

2. Make the agenda visible, by writing it up on a blackboard or flip-chart.

3. Allow 'last minute' items to be put on the agenda at the beginning of a meeting.

4. Discuss with the group the order in which items should be taken, or establish a rationale for the priorities you set.

5. Allocate time so that all issues receive an appropriate amount of attention.

These points are basic but are often overlooked or ignored. Unless attention is paid to them, it is unlikely a successful meeting will emerge.

Stages in Business Meetings

The second major factor regarding procedure in meetings concerns the steps taken during discussion. All those attending a meeting require a common language and procedure to communicate effectively about the conduct, as opposed to the content, of meetings. It is useful to ask in meetings 'where are we now?', or 'what are we presently doing?'

It is suggested that there are six main stages during any meeting. At each stage, it is possible to be discussing at least two aspects of any issue under consideration. In all, therefore, there are twelve possible levels of procedural discussion at meetings. These facets of business meetings are shown in Fig. 16.1.

Stages		Process phases
1.	Aims	Objectives
		Purpose
2.	Problem diagnosis	Resources
		Constraints
3.	Solutions generation	Means
		Ends
4.	Action choice	Criteria
		Method
5.	Implementation	Organization
		Relationships
6.	Evaluation	Subjective
		Objective

Fig. 16.1

It is not uncommon therefore to find some members discussing policy objectives relating to what the meeting is trying to achieve, while others are talking about the purpose or reason for pursuing such objectives.

As a meeting goes on, it is possible for people to make contributions which belong to different stages of the discussion. For example, if one member says 'I think we ought to go ahead immediately and develop the new product and have it on the market by the New Year', this is a stage 4 contribution. This person, having weighed the information before him, is prepared to make an action choice. Meanwhile another member may still be at stage 3: 'I don't think we should be so hasty in rushing into a decision. It seems to me that we could go about this in a different way. Let us consider the other alternatives.' This is a solution generation comment, whereby the individual wishes to consider the range of solutions before making a choice.

Another may still be at stage 2: 'I'm not sure that we have diagnosed the problem correctly. Is it true that our existing product is obsolete? Maybe there are other causes for the decline in sales. I think we need to get more information on this before proceeding further.' This member does not wish to consider solutions until he feels he has correctly diagnosed the problem. His concern is that he may develop solutions that are irrelevant in the real problem.

Another member may still be at stage 1: 'Look, it's no use talking about sales of this product until we have finally decided what our policy is to be for the next five years. I feel there are considerable changes taking place in the market for this product. We have therefore got to decide whether we are to continue in this market. If so, we must decide how much money we can afford to allocate to this product given our other priorities.' Clearly, this person is questioning the validity of operating in this market area and wishes to get the members to consider the policy.

If a meeting is being conducted at different stages or levels, it is likely that little progress will be made. Each of the members in the above case study was trying to control the ground upon which discussion should take place and each was at a different stage. Just as people can be distant geographically, so it is possible for them to be distant mentally. Both geographical and mental distance make communication difficult. The essential thing is to know how to recognize when people are talking at different stages of the problem, and when members are mentally distant from one another. The manager must be able to do this and be able to guide people to concentrate on one area at a time.

Guideline: When people are discussing at different stages, seek to return the conversation to the stage at which the difference first emerged.

Personal Contributions to Discussions

If we take the issues identified in Fig. 16.1 and look more closely at them, it gives us some guide to the sort of behaviour that needs to be engaged in at various stages of any meeting. The six stages of any meeting demand personal contributions in each of the areas listed below. It is usual that most of us have more ability in some of these stages than others.

1. POLICY AIMS

The extent to which a person helps develop objectives, and the purpose for engaging in a work task activity

As indicated above, it is vital in all meetings for consideration to be given to:

1. What are we trying to achieve?
2. Why are we trying to achieve it?

If these issues are not clarified and basic agreement gained, then a meeting is likely to be ineffective. Clearly, it is not always possible to reach complete agreement on objectives and purpose. However, even in, say, union–management negotiations, there are vital elements of common ground which need to be clarified. For example, the union's objective will be to get a 10 per cent wage increase. The company offers 5 per cent. The danger is that both sides will haggle over these separate objectives, rather than consider the purpose they both have in common: how to increase wealth and establish means for sharing it. The move towards productivity or collective bargaining represents a change in thinking to look at conflicting objectives in the context of a wider purpose which may have grounds for mutual satisfaction.

Let us examine another meeting, where concern over the effectiveness of advertising was expressed. The managing director of a company said it was necessary to spend more on promotions as sales were low. Questions were raised about the cost of this and the likely benefit. The meeting was getting bogged down, when the sales manager asked: 'What are we trying to do with our advertising?' He was derided for asking such a basic question when everyone saw the objective as that of increasing sales. However, he persisted: 'Look, I'm not questioning the objective, I'm questioning the purpose of our activity. If our objective is to increase sales, what is the purpose? If it is to increase profit, we should look at other solutions. Well, we could achieve that by pursuing complementary objectives such as cutting costs of production, bulk buying, reducing credit facilities, setting a higher or lower price. The question I'm raising is what is the ultimate purpose of achieving more sales through increased advertising?' The effect of this contribution on those present was to widen the discussion and open up alternatives that had not previously been considered.

Guideline: Objectives and purpose need to be discussed in depth. Too often, they are skipped over and problems occur as a result.

2. PROBLEM DIAGNOSIS

The extent to which a person exhibits knowledge *and* skills *in identifying and overcoming a problem to help the group achieve its task*

Having defined the policy objectives and purpose, it is necessary to consider problems that are likely to emerge. In this context, problems refer both to resources as well as to deviations from standard.

Closed-Ended Problems

For example, a problem may emerge because something that was previously in working order, such as a machine, has broken down. Here there is a deviation in the function of a given product. It is presumably possible to discover the reason for this deviation, by examining the *cause* of the breakdown. However, in some situations where a deficiency occurs people treat the *symptom* rather than the cause. For example, in medical work it is often difficult to know exactly what causes ulcers. Doctors therefore treat the symptoms by reducing the acid level in the stomach or even removing the ulcer surgically. The critical point is to know whether the problem can be tackled successfully by removing the symptoms. Will the problem still remain? If so, it is necessary to clearly identify the causes. This is often best done in a meeting by writing down on a board, visible to all, the problem, listing underneath possible factors producing the problem. These can then be analysed as either causative and/or symptomatic factors.

Where there is a problem that involves deviation from an established standard, then we shall call this a *closed-ended problem*. A machine breakdown would be a closed-ended problem, as the solution would involve getting the machine back to the standard previously established and at which it operates efficiently.

The procedure for resolving such problems is relatively straightforward. It involves identifying:

1. What is the standard to which we must work.
2. When the deviation from this standard occurred.
3. Where the deviation occurred.
4. How the deviation occurred.
5. Why the deviation occurred.
6. What is necessary to be done to regain the standard.

Open-Ended Problems

The other major type of problem is found in a different type of situation. Here there is no accepted standard from which a deviation can be measured. The problem concerns the necessary resources, such as materials or information, to achieve the objectives and purpose set. This problem is becoming more important in modern organizations where people have to resolve problems which require contributions from various professional groups, all of whom know a part of the problem, but not the whole issue. Hard thinking needs to be done in asking the appropriate questions. The problem in this area is, 'In what direction do we need to go?' It will occur whenever there is an open-ended situation where there is no clearcut, standard answer.

Typical of such situations are in the formulation of advertising slogans, in the preparation of long-term plans, in the establishing of a new training course, in setting of policy, etc. The acquisition of resources in such situations is a problem which is often difficult to measure.

Let us consider an example. The director of operations in a large company wants to increase the efficiency of his organization. He therefore calls together the purchasing manager, the production manager, the sales manager, and the distribution manager. He tells them that the company policy is to cut costs and improve service to customers. The problem is how it should be done. The purchasing manager says that if he receives notice of production requirements earlier he can buy in bulk and gain discount savings. Others say this would cause a stock-holding problem. The production manager says that if he could produce a range of four products on long runs then costs could be lowered. The sales manager argues this would reduce service to customers; he feels that a wider range of products would help customer service, but this is opposed by the production manager as being impossible with existing machines and staff. Clearly, many problems are associated with adopting the policy of cutting costs and improving service. There is no easy answer.

A central problem is that the standard has not been set. There is only a general requirement that costs and service be improved. The group therefore, has an open-ended problem on its hands. Each member has a different definition of what constitutes lower costs and improved service. Therefore, an initial step is to identify this joint problem and narrow down the issue. What criteria or yardstick constitute a measuring rod? At what level should costs be set, and what level of service should be aimed for? Once these issues have been established the problem becomes manageable. At this stage, members can begin to share knowledge and ideas for the problem has been defined.

There are numerous situations like this one where the difficulty is in defining the problem, so that everyone knows what is being sought and can direct their knowledge and skill to that end. The art of problem diagnosis, sometimes called 'problem finding', is often more than half the battle towards problem solving. Once problems have been clearly defined, the next stage of solution generation should be started.

Guideline: Identify whether you are dealing with an open- or closed-ended problem. If it is closed-ended, you will be working within a preset standard or range of criteria. These should be established and shared before problem diagnosis begins. If it is open-ended, your prime task is to define the standards and criteria within which the problem must be assessed before problem diagnosis begins.

3. SOLUTIONS GENERATION

(a) *Idea generation: The extent to which a person initiates ideas for the group to consider in relation to the task. This involves the generation of alternatives*

Good ideas for solving problems need to be made public. It is important, therefore, to provide the appropriate conditions to enable people with ideas to come forward. One method, now reasonably well accepted, is the 'brain-storming session'. Here, people put forward ideas, which are written for all to see on a board. During the generation phase, no one criticizes any of the ideas. Various other methods have been developed, using analogies, metaphors, word association, and other approaches to aid the creative process. However, the major block to idea generation is the failure of a group to explore new ideas. Too often they are killed at birth. It is important therefore to separate idea generation from idea development.

(*b*) *Idea development: The extent to which a person builds on and develops an idea to aid the group achieve its task*
This is a skill that is not widely recognized, mainly because the person playing this role is helping another to extend his ideas. He may do this by asking a question: 'Tell me more about . . . .' Alternatively, he may para-phrase the other person's point as an invitation for him to continue. He may, of course, add to the preceding comment or progress the conversation by suggesting an amendment to the proposed solution. This is called 'building on ideas'.

The important point about idea generation and idea development is the need to seek as many solutions as possible. Often solutions of inferior quality are implemented because the search for other possible solutions ceases once a 'reasonable' answer has been found. Once a number of solutions is available, it is possible to see if a combination of them in varying degrees gives a more appropriate answer than any single one by itself.

The critical test for all solutions is that they must have:
1. Sufficient technical quality to resolve the problem.
2. A level of acceptability from those implementing the solution.

The use of this formulation in relation to a given problem is again best done on a blackboard or group chart, so that everyone sees the progress of the discussion. The presentation in a visual form can be done as indicated in the following example.

A manager got a group of his subordinates together and told them he was concerned with their record of lateness. He said he was not going to single individuals out for attention. Instead, he wished the group to meet and develop solutions to resolving the problem. He asked the group to bring forward as many solutions as possible and to let him see these ideas in three days' time. He also indicated that at the next meeting he would bring forward the solutions, and then the whole group could make a decision on what to do, given that the solutions eventually chosen must solve the problem and be acceptable both to himself and the group.

At the meeting, three days later, the staff and the manager put forward their respective solutions on a flipchart.

STAFF SOLUTIONS	MANAGER'S SOLUTIONS
Open the works half an hour later and reduce working week by $2\frac{1}{2}$ hours.	Deduct half an hour's pay for each 15 minutes a person is late.
Arrange special transport to and from railway station.	Work a shift system.
Allow each department to decide on its own time-keeping arrangements.	Start as at present, have shorter lunch break, finish earlier.
	Reward good time-keeping.

These solutions were discussed in depth. The emphasis of the discussion was for a mutual exchange of information on each other's solutions. The staff asked questions of the manager regarding his solutions. The sort of questions that were raised were 'Why do you suggest deducting pay from people who are late?' and 'What exactly do you mean by a shift system?' Likewise, the manager inquired of the staff 'How would special transport to and from the railway station help?' and 'What effect on productivity will it have if we cut $2\frac{1}{2}$ hours off the working week?' The aim of these questions was to clarify the propositions and gain understanding of the points being put forward.

In this process, there is always a danger that people will close down the conversation by asking a 'leading question', i.e., one which implies that the person asking it wants to make a point rather than get information. A leading question usually involves either a veto or an alternative proposition. For example, in the above meeting someone said to the manager 'Don't you think that penalizing the latecomers by imposing a fine on them will make them so annoyed that they will deliberately go slow in order to get their own back?' This is a question that implies a rejection of the idea being put forward.

To provide an opportunity for such points to be made, each side should be asked in an open-ended way what comments they have on the other's proposals. This, again, is a sharing of views, and allows for a response to be made clarifying any points of misinterpretation. At the completion of this stage, both sides should feel they have:

1. Put over their proposals.
2. Explained their proposals, which have been understood though not necessarily accepted.
3. Heard the other side's proposals.
4. Clarified these proposals through questioning, while not necessarily accepting them.

Once this had been achieved, it is appropriate to move on to the next stage of the problem-solving process.

4. ACTION CHOICE

The extent to which a person seeks to make a choice from the available altern-atives and influence others to accept a decision that will resolve the problem

This stage is often extremely difficult. It involves assessing the available solutions and making a choice which will not only solve the problem, but be acceptable to those who will have to implement the decision.

In the above example, the proposed solutions were in the main in-compatible. The staff's ideas were not acceptable to the manager, and vice versa. This is not unusual. With interpersonal problems of this kind, it is rare that any one solution will resolve the problems. The reason for generating and considering as many solutions as possible is to provide a range of choice from which a composite solution may emerge.

In the above example, the discussion moved into the action choice stage when a staff member combined some of the ideas of both the manager and his staff. He said: 'We would like each department to have its own time-keeping arrangements, and you have suggested a shift system. Maybe if we put these ideas together we could solve the problem. If we established a system where everyone had to work between 10.00AM and 4.00PM, perhaps we could arrange a shift system in each department to cover the period between 8.00AM and 10.00AM, and 4.00PM and 5.30PM. This may also enable us to reduce the number of working hours per week, provided productivity continued as at present.'

This information became the basis for a decision, which was accepted and developed. The important thing was that the formulation met what both sides felt to be their interest. This, of course, does not always happen.

It is important, therefore, at the action choice situation, to decide how the decision is to be taken. The major approaches available are:

1. **Colleague decision**—unanimous agreement among all participants.

2. **Committee decision**—a decision which if not unanimous will be decided by the majority principle through a vote.

3. **Negotiated decision**—a decision which if not unanimous will be decided by bargaining and exchange, ultimately related to the power of the participating sides.

4. **Command decision**—a decision taken by the leader or superior in the meeting which he believes he has the authority to enforce, even if participants disagree with his view.

5. **Consultative decision**—a decision by the manager to listen to the views of his colleagues or subordinates, and where appropriate give inform-ation, but reserve the right to withhold judgement until such time as the manager feels it right to take action.

In previous chapters, we examined these approaches to decision making in more detail. Here it is sufficient to indicate that, at the action choice stage, managers should be aware of what the alternatives are and the type of decision they wish to make.

5. IMPLEMENTATION

The extent to which a person facilitates the successful completion of the task within the set criteria, by establishing an organization structure, managing time, costs, and people to achieve objectives

Although the issues at this stage will be decided in a meeting, the implementation stage invariably takes place at a time and place separate from where the decisions are taken. The implementation stage, therefore, involves identifying:

1. What has to be achieved.
2. What time scale is necessary.
3. What budget is allowed.
4. Who is accountable for given tasks.
5. Who will work with whom, and what the role relationships will be.

The implementation stage depends heavily for its success on planning. It may involve developing network diagrams to indicate what jobs have to be done and at what time. The essence of implementation involves people knowing their task and the constraints and resources within which the task must be done. All these things can be discussed and plans developed in a meeting.

One approach to implementation planning has been through management by objectives. This approach has emphasized the necessity for people to discuss with their manager and colleagues the objectives they are to pursue. In this way, an effort to clarify what each person in a team is doing has been sought so that mistakes will not occur due to duplication or inadequate task coverage. Sometimes this has been no more than a paper planning exercise, although in some companies the method has been found to be particularly helpful in the organization of work planning. Beyond the planning stage, however, success depends on day to day task management.

6. EVALUATION

The extent to which a person facilitates an assessment of performance and generates information related to improving further action

For a task to be completed effectively, continual evaluation of its implementation is required. The sixth stage in the process is to review or monitor the progress of the decisions taken. On some tasks, formal review periods may be built in. For example, some managers meet with their staff regularly each Monday morning to review progress and iron out any difficulties.

Evaluation can take place on two levels.

Task evaluation   This is an assessment of how far the task objectives have been achieved. Did the raw materials arrive in the right quantity and quality and on time? Were production quotas met? To what extent have sales targets been achieved? These objectives have to be evaluated to assess the factors involved in the work.

Relationships evaluation   This is an assessment of how effectively people work together in the organization. Such an evaluation examines things like personal performance, team work, leadership style, employee motivation, interpersonal communication. This form of evaluation is often done in appraisal interviews, management by objective meetings, work group reviews, and so on. It is probably more difficult than task evaluation as it involves assessing people rather than things. However, it is a vital part of any evaluation procedure. The ideas expressed in the previous pages will give some indication of issues to be aware of when engaged in such evaluation.

The important thing about any evaluation procedure is that it be aimed at improving the existing situation. If the evaluation is done merely to keep records, to punish or deflate people's efforts, then it will fail. All evaluation should be related to the future, not the past. Evaluation should be less a judgement, and more a supportive, developmental exercise, with the focus on bringing about improvement both at the technical task and behavioural relationships level.

Managerial Meetings and the Stages of Operation

Now the above stages may look rather formal and forbidding. That is not the intention. The stages are only an outline of the steps that can be gone through in a meeting, and there are a number of meetings where these stages will not necessarily apply. For example, the *advisory* meeting could end at stage 1. The manager may come along and simply state company policy. He does not wish to consider problems, or solutions, or action. His intention is to inform. Likewise, in a *command* meeting, the meeting could finish at stage 5. Again, some meetings may be held where the participants feel they know the policy and problems and start at stage 3 in considering solutions. There is no set pattern of having to follow through all the stages one by one. Nevertheless, in most meetings, stages 1 to 5 will usually be implemented, even if it is not in a sequential order.

The issue of the agenda is therefore only a guideline. If you are holding a *command* meeting, it is unlikely you will allow everyone to come along and add to the agenda. The guidelines on the agenda proposals apply more to the *advisory* committee, *colleague* and *negotiation* meetings. The important point is that the approaches developed and used must be in accord with the type of meeting you are organizing and the objectives to be achieved.

Conclusion

These guidelines are only useful if applied. Problems have been diagnosed, and solutions put forward. The third and crucial element is the extent to which the ideas are put into action. That decision rests with you, the reader.

Action is the most difficult thing to carry out in the managerial problem-solving process. The ideas outlined here may not work the first time; a period of time may be required to have an effect. In managerial problem solving, there are few easy ways to success. What is absolutely necessary is the skill to talk with others in groups, to resolve problems, and to seek opportunities. This demands high interpersonal communication skills and, above all, knowing when and how to be problem-, solution-, or action-centred.

Summary
A. In this chapter, attention has been drawn to some guidelines on the conduct of business meetings and has included:
- The development of a visible, flexible agenda.
- The stages of business meetings.
- The summary guidelines for action.
- The relation between the type of meeting and the conduct of business meetings.

B. In particular, the chapter should enable the manager to:
- Develop a procedure for business meetings.
- Establish a problem-solving climate.
- Recognize the six stages of business meetings.
- Draw attention to the fact that people may be discussing aims, diagnosis, solutions, action choice, implementation, and evaluation concurrently.

C. In considering the issues raised, a manager should ask himself:
- How far are my meetings effective?
- To what extent should people attending meetings be made aware of the stages to be gone through?
- To what extent should the agenda be made 'open'?
- What do I need to do to improve my skills and knowledge in the areas identified?

GLOSSARY OF TERMS

Business meetings The six major stages of business meetings identified have been called: policy aims; problem diagnosis; solution generation; action choice; implementation and evaluation.

Closed-ended problems Problems that exist within defined limits, and to which there is a predetermined answer. Good examples are a jigsaw puzzle, and mending a broken machine.

Conversational responses There are five main responses:
- Aggressive – attack;
- Defensive – defend;
- Regressive – withdraw;
- Fixative – repeat;
- Supportive – help or support.

Conversational seduction The process of moving from one issue to another during conversation, so that the original issue is bypassed and not dealt with.

Cornering The process used to negate the ideas being developed by another person by countering each point he makes with an objection.

Group problem solving (GPS) The nature of problem-solving behaviour in group situations, involving both the interaction process between people and the structure of the meeting itself, including the type of meeting and the stages.

Interpersonal problem solving (IPS)   The interaction process between people when resolving problems.

Interpersonal problem-solving distance   The gap between people in discussions on various issues. It is analogous to geographical distance, only it is measured in conversational terms. The same idea is expressed in the terms *mental distance* and *conversational distance*.

Managerial help   An attempt by a manager to give assistance to another person on matters relating to his work.

Managerial problem solving   The behaviour of a manager in resolving problems with particular reference to his interactions with others involved.

Managerial problem-solving approaches   Types of approaches include:
- Consultative – emphasizes the approach to problems through the asking of questions and giving of information where the questioner and information giver controls the conversation.
- Reflective – emphasizes the approach to problems through listening to the other's viewpoints, so that the other person controls the conversation.
- Negotiative – emphasizes the approach to solutions based on bargaining.
- Prescriptive – emphasizes the approach to solutions based on suggesting remedies for other people.
- Directive – emphasizes the approach to solutions based on telling others what to do.

Meetings   The types of meetings dealt with are:
- Advisory – a meeting for the exchange of information.
- Committee – a meeting of representatives deciding issues by the vote.
- Colleague – a meeting of people with similar status deciding issues unanimously.
- Command – a meeting called to give instructions.
- Negotiation – a meeting between people with different objectives but willing to settle issues through bargaining.

Open-ended problems   Problems that do not have preset answers but require criteria to be established by the problem solver as to various issues. An example is setting a budget.

Problem-centred orientation   The approach of a person who concentrates on problem diagnosis by using consultative or reflective behaviour.

Problem-solving approaches   Behaviour that seeks to generate information relating to the task, so that a decision can be made and action taken.

Problem-solving mix   The relationship between the availability of solutions and the clarity of problem diagnosis.

PSA cycle   The relationship between problem diagnosis, solution development, and action implementation.

Punishment-centred approaches   Behaviour that allocates or attributes blame, sarcasm, implication, or accusation to others when something goes wrong.

Self-fulfilling prophecy   A statement or act that tends to foretell the development of subsequent events.

Social distance   The gap between people in terms of status, prestige, and respect. Also known as the *status differential*.

Solution-centred orientation   The approach of a person who concentrates on solution development by using directive, prescriptive, or negotiative behaviour.

INDEX

PRINTED IN GREAT BRITAIN BY OFFSET LITHOGRAPHY BY
BILLING AND SONS LTD., GUILDFORD AND LONDON